BEYOND THE STARS:
EMBRACING COSMIC LAWS TO INTENTIONALLY CREATE A LIFE OF FULFILMENT

BEYOND THE STARS: EMBRACING COSMIC LAWS TO INTENTIONALLY CREATE A LIFE OF FULFILMENT

WOURNAL YOUR JOURNEY

(No, it's not a typo. Wournal is a portmanteau of the words workbook and journal. I hope you like it!)

VICTORIA GREEN

GET YOUR FREE GIFT!

I want to make your personal transformation as easy as possible for you. If you would like a free ebook which is a downloadable, printable workbook—because I do love a good workbook—then pop the link below into your browser and download your copy today.

You can get a copy by visiting:
https://victoriagreen-lifecoach.com/workbook

DEDICATION

In loving memory of:

Ieuan Phillip (Griff) Griffiths was a constant presence
in my life as I grew up. I miss you, and I love you.

Stanley Green, without whom I would not be
on this earth, I forgive and love you.

OUR DEEPEST FEAR

OUR DEEPEST FEAR IS **NOT** THAT WE ARE INADEQUATE
OUR DEEPEST FEAR IS THAT **WE ARE** POWERFUL
BEYOND MEASURE
IT IS **OUR LIGHT**, NOT OUR DARKNESS
THAT MOST **FRIGHTENS US.**

WE ASK OURSELVES
WHO **AM I** TO BE **BRILLIANT**, GORGEOUS, **TALENTED,**
FABULOUS,
ACTUALLY, **WHO ARE YOU NOT TO BE?**
YOU ARE A CHILD OF THE **UNIVERSE.**

YOUR **PLAYING SMALL**
DOES NOT SERVE THE WORLD
THERE'S NOTHING **ENLIGHTENED** ABOUT SHRINKING
SO THAT OTHER PEOPLE WON'T FEEL INSECURE
AROUND YOU

WE ARE ALL MEANT TO **SHINE**
AS CHILDREN DO
WE WERE BORN TO **MANIFEST**
THE GLORY OF THE **UNIVERSE** THAT IS WITHIN US.

IT'S NOT JUST IN SOME OF US
IT'S IN **EVERYONE.**

AND AS WE LET OUR OWN **LIGHT SHINE**
WE **UNCONSCIOUSLY** GIVE OTHER PEOPLE
PERMISSION TO DO THE SAME
AS WE'RE **LIBERATED FROM OUR OWN FEAR**
OUR PRESENCE AUTOMATICALLY **LIBERATES OTHERS.**

—A MODIFIED POEM BY MARIANNE WILLIAMSON

TABLE OF CONTENTS

Section One
Setting the Foundations of Manifestation

Section Two
The Toolkit

SECTION ONE
SETTING THE FOUNDATIONS OF MANIFESTATION

'Educating the mind without educating the heart is no education at all.'
—Aristotle

THE UNIVERSAL LAWS

*'Faith is taking the first step even when you
don't see the whole staircase.'*
—Martin Luther King Jr

Unless you have lived under a rock for the last fifteen years or more, you will surely have heard about the Law of Attraction, right? For me, and perhaps for many of those reading this book, it came about with the release of the film *The Secret* in 2006. Over the years, I have tried many times to manifest material things in my life, but with limited success. I didn't know back then that there were more Universal Laws that we should live by. Without understanding, acknowledging, and respecting these other laws, our manifestation success will continue to be limited.

For decades now, 'New Thought' leaders have been influential in introducing and spreading the word about these Universal Laws to a much broader and more varied audience. They have emphasised the need for positive thinking, discussed the role of karma in our lives, and explained how the Law of Attraction can manifest our heart's desires. Furthermore, they have informed us of how our thoughts and actions have shaped our reality, good or bad!

Until recently, I failed to appreciate that this notion began hundreds of years ago by great philosophers, teachers, and scientists. These teachings have been passed down through ancient civilisations such as the Egyptians, Greeks, and Hindus, who all believed in these cosmic principles. Humans have thought these laws govern our lives and the Universe for centuries. Greek philosophers, such as Pythagoras, Plato, and Socrates, believed in interconnectedness, or the Law of Divine Oneness. Eastern philosophers, those who follow the teachings of Hinduism and Buddhism, have long taught the lessons of karma, which is related to the Law of Compensation.

Since learning about the work of the late great Dolores Cannon, who died in 2014, I have come to realise that she, too, added further validation to these Universal Laws through her extensive research and numerous experiences accessing the subconscious to report on lost knowledge, or indeed, knowledge that wasn't known at all. Dolores spent many decades researching thousands of past lives. She directly contacted the subconscious/ higher-self/oversoul, whatever name you wish to call it, to gain detailed information about the Universe and the spirit realm. Dolores teaches us that Earth is just a school where we must learn our lessons, and she informs us we are here to experience what it is like to be a human being. She, too, reported that we are all one and that each of us is on a karmic cycle. Her advice to us was to repay and rid ourselves of karma during this lifetime, and she warned that without repaying it now, we would have to come back and do our lessons all over again and with the same people! Scary thought, eh?

I will be honest; some people I do *not* want to incarnate with again will remain anonymous! I'm sure that resonates with some of you, too.

As humans, we need to regularly remind ourselves that we are more spiritual beings than physical ones and that it takes a master manifester to get onto this planet in the first place. We must remember *who* we are, *what* we are, and *why* we chose to incarnate onto this Earth at this specific time. Dolores said we are all here to learn how to manipulate energy and to create. She further suggests that all of us can create *anything* we want in our lives; there are *no* limits unless you have put those limits on yourself. First and foremost, though, we need to know *what* we want to create.[1]

THE PURPOSE OF THIS BOOK

'You are not a drop in the ocean … you are the ocean.'
—Rumi

This book aims to help you raise your awareness of the twelve Universal Laws, acknowledge them, understand them, and respect them so that you can do your utmost to live by them. In doing so, you would play a part in raising the planet's vibration to benefit us all. You will rid yourself of any limiting beliefs that no longer serve you, and subsequently, your happiness will increase, and you will manifest, with ease, anything that your heart desires.

If the work we do together were spread far and wide, I would like the world to become a better place for everyone to live. This is a *big* ambition, but through our collective consciousness, each of us doing our part to help and serve others and intentionally focusing on self-development and growth, we could all help raise the planet's vibration. I *genuinely* believe everyone can achieve much more love, harmony, and happiness in and for the world. How fantastic would that be?

The twelve Universal Laws are the blueprint for understanding the mysteries of life. They act as a guide for our behaviour, to which we should harness our true life values. Without incorporating

---

[1]　'About Dolores & QHHT®,' QHHT Official Website, March 24, 2024, https://www.qhhtofficial.com/about-us/.

the full suite of laws into our lives, we will continue to suffer, be unhappy and unsuccessful, and inadvertently gather karma as we navigate this life on Earth.

Deepak Chopra stated, 'When you discover your essential nature and know who you are, because *knowing* is the ability to fulfil any dream you have, because you are the eternal possibility, the immeasurable potential of all that was, is and ever will be'.[2]

My ambition for this book is to provide you, the reader, with a more detailed account of each of the twelve Universal Laws and to provide an opportunity for you to reflect, assess, and 'wournal' about how you currently use them, and how you can use them more effectively in the future by using a method known as the 5Ws and 1H. There are many exercises for you to complete in the book, from understanding and overcoming your self-limiting beliefs to an introduction to visualisation and positive affirmations, and much more.

PURSUE YOUR DREAMS

*'All our dreams can come true if we have t
he courage to pursue them.'*
—Walt Disney

My plan for this book was to bring to your attention as many tools as possible so that you don't need to look for them. I hope you find all of them useful. My wish for you is that you can enrich your life and those around you as you embrace the laws and learn how to incorporate them into your daily life. Through leading by example, you unconsciously encourage others to do the same.

Ultimately, I want this book to positively impact and improve your happiness so you can truly become who you are meant to

---

[2]   Deepak Chopra, The Seven Laws of Success, accessed June 14, 2024, https://archive.org/details/deepak-chopra-the-7-laws-of-success.

be. The bonus here is that you may rid yourself of some of the karma you have gathered throughout your life—although I can't guarantee this!

In the following chapters, we will discuss the tools I have found the most helpful for creating a better reality for myself. You will learn how to:

- Define and understand the Twelve Universal Laws and how they apply to manifestation.
- Set goals using the 5Ws and 1H, SMART goal setting, and the GROW model.
- Complete the Wheel of Life if you're overwhelmed with life and goals.
- Address your self-limiting beliefs and explore the Looping Thought Ladder.
- Express your gratitude graciously.
- Write a letter to the Universe.
- Improve your visualisation technique.
- Integrate positive affirmations using the 3-6-9 method.
- Discover the principles of cognitive behavioural therapy (CBT) to overcome self-sabotage, imposter syndrome, or negative self-talk.

The toolkit can be used in whichever way best serves you. You can dip in and out of the tools you like, skip the ones you don't want or plough through the lot. If you're going to jump to the Universal Laws and return to other previous sections later, that's okay, too.

Remember, though, you should reflect on your journey and document how far you have come, and these wournal tools will help you do just that. Before all that and without further ado, let's look at a brief overview of the Universal Laws and how they impact our manifestation success. So, if you're sitting comfortably, let's get started!

UNIVERSAL LAWS AND MANIFESTATION

*'You are never too old to set another
goal or to dream a new dream.'*
—C.S Lewis

Why do some people effortlessly attract success, abundance, and happiness? Is it luck, or is it coincidence? The simple answer to this is that it's neither luck nor coincidence. It's about understanding how to harness the power of *all* twelve laws and how to integrate them fully into our lives. While most of us continue to only pay attention to the most famous law, the Law of Attraction, we do so in complete ignorance of the other eleven laws that govern the Universe in which we live. Focusing on one law while neglecting the others creates an imbalance within us and the Universe.

The laws are interconnected and entwined, each building on the other. Therefore, we must understand each law and how they work harmoniously together for our greater good and maximum effect. Understanding these laws better equips us to play the game of life, and working with them will bring about positive change, higher vibrations, and amazing things and experiences into our lives.

The realm of Universal Laws and how they are intricately connected to the art of manifestation is fascinating. Whether you believe in these principles or not, there is no denying their impact on our lives when applied consciously and with intention and purpose.

This will give you a taste of what the Universal Laws offer and their importance to manifestation. We will dive into each of them in a much deeper way later. For now, though, let's look at an overview. So, fasten your seatbelts and prepare to discover a new way of approaching life that aligns with these powerful forces governing our Universe.

THE TWELVE UNIVERSAL LAWS

'Nothing is impossible, the very word itself says "I'm Possible."'
—Audrey Hepburn

Universal laws are the fundamental principles that govern the workings of our Universe. They are the invisible forces that shape our reality and determine what we attract into our lives. These laws are not just abstract concepts; they have been observed and studied by scientists, philosophers, and spiritual teachers throughout history.

One key aspect of Universal Laws is their consistency. They work behind the scenes to create a harmonious balance within our lives and the Universe. They can be seen as guidelines explaining how energy flows and impacts our lives.

Many of the laws we will discuss may resonate with you, and the premise behind some of them will be familiar, I'm sure, but you may not have been aware that these were considered Universal Laws. Understanding these laws gives us insight into how things manifest in our lives, both positive and negative. These laws encompass various principles.

1. **The Law of Divine Oneness:** One key aspect of understanding Universal Laws is realising that everything in the Universe is connected. Every thought, action, and emotion we experience impacts our lives and world. This interconnectedness forms the basis for how Universal Laws work and is the premise of the primary law of all laws.

2. **The Law of Vibration:** This is another essential principle emphasising that everything in the Universe vibrates at a frequency, often undetected by the naked eye. Our thoughts, emotions, and beliefs emit vibrations

that resonate with similar frequencies in the external world.

3. **The Law of Correspondence:** This relates to how your internal world is mirrored in your external world or reality. If you transform your inner world, your reality changes in accordance. This law decrees that one is all, and all is one.

4. **The Law of Attraction:** This law states that like attracts like. It suggests that whatever energy or vibration we send into the Universe will be reflected to us in kind.

5. **The Law of Inspired Action:** Recognising that manifestation doesn't occur solely through wishful thinking, hopefulness, or passive daydreaming is essential. It requires active participation in collaboration with the other Universal Laws that focus on raising our vibration.

6. **The Law of Perpetual Transmutation of Energy:** This law states that energy is constantly evolving or fluctuating. It makes perfect sense because the Law of Vibration states that everything is energy, and the Law of Attraction states that like attracts like. Your energy is always moving towards high vibration (positivity) or low vibration (negativity). So, your job is to monitor your vibration alignment and focus on better-feeling thoughts when necessary.

7. **The Law of Cause and Effect:** It proposes that every action has a consequence; for every cause, there is an effect, and for every effect, there is a cause. This law reminds us to take responsibility for our choices because they shape our reality.

8. **The Law of Compensation:** This law encourages us to consistently offer kindness to our fellow human beings. Taking inspired action towards our goals while providing kindness, positivity, and help to others amplifies the

manifestation process and its success as the Universe returns these blessings to you.

9. **The Law of Relativity:** This law states that everything is relative because we all perceive reality in our own way. This explains why two people can experience the same situation but have different perspectives. Understanding this law helps you prioritise inner peace over defending the truth because 'truth' is relative, anyway.

10. **The Law of Polarity:** This law states that everything in life has an opposite. For every problem, there's a solution. For every obstacle, there's an opportunity. This law gives birth to new desires when manifesting. Every time you experience something you don't want, this law points out that the thing you wish to exist is just waiting to manifest in your life.

11. **The Law of Rhythm:** Cycles are a natural part of the Universe. Just like the four seasons, your life has seasons, too. Surrender to the flow of life and let your inner wisdom guide your thoughts, words, and actions.

12. **The Law of Gender:** Life works best when divine masculine and divine feminine energies align. The divine feminine represents the part of our consciousness that connects us to qualities like intuition, feeling, emotions, creativity, and spirituality. This divine feminine energy is the opposite of the divine masculine, which connects us to qualities like logic, authority, confidence, objectivity, and action-taking. One thing to note is that one is equal to the other. The divine feminine and the divine masculine must work harmoniously to create solutions for the highest good.

These Universal Laws are at play in our lives every day. Understanding these principles allows us to navigate life *consciously* rather than being mere passengers on a journey.

MANIFESTATION

'Believe you can, and you're halfway there.'
—Theodore Roosevelt

Now, how do these Universal Laws relate to manifestation? Universal laws are timeless and apply to all aspects of life, from nature to human behaviour. These laws are not artificial rules but rather inherent truths that exist in the fabric of reality.

We must genuinely understand Universal Laws and recognise their role in shaping our experiences through manifestation. Manifestation refers to bringing something into reality by aligning our thoughts, beliefs, and actions with our desires. By applying these laws effectively, we can consciously manifest positive outcomes in various areas of life: relationships, career success, health improvement, love, and much more.

In essence, by understanding the principles of Universal Laws and aligning ourselves with positive intentions, we can harness the power of manifestation to create a life filled with abundance, joy, and success. When we consciously choose thoughts and beliefs that support our desires while releasing any negative limiting patterns or beliefs, we open up space for these desires to manifest in our lives.

Incorporating practices like affirmations and visualisation can further enhance our ability to manifest. By consistently affirming positive statements about what we want to attract into our lives and visualising ourselves experiencing those desires as though they are already fulfilled and in vivid detail, we send powerful signals to the Universe that we are ready for change and willing to participate actively to make it happen.

It's worth noting that successful manifestation isn't always immediate or linear; there will be delays along the way due to factors beyond our control, and this serves us well. We wouldn't want the first desire we think about to arrive at our front door miraculously. Imagine, one day, you are fooling around with your friend, and you say, 'Oh, I'd love to have an alien come for tea!'

Next thing you know, 'Ding dong!' The doorbell rings, and standing there is Nigel, a tall green alien from the planet Glog. For clarity, I don't *think* there is a planet called 'Glog'. However, I cannot guarantee there are no aliens called 'Nigel'! You can see from this silly example that this time delay is positive because it allows us to change our minds and readjust our thoughts to what we *really* want to manifest. Be clear from the outset so you don't get any unexpected visitors from the planet Glog.

The connection between the Universal Laws and manifestation runs deep. By understanding these principles, aligning ourselves with positive intentions, taking inspired action, and practising gratitude and kindness, we can harness the power of manifestation and transform our lives for the better.

CHAPTER 1

UNIVERSAL LAW #1: THE LAW OF DIVINE ONENESS

*'The most difficult thing is the decision to
act; the rest is merely tenacity.'*
—Amelia Earhart

To comprehend the Twelve Laws of the Universe, take a moment to envision the mesmerising planet Earth, a celestial body suspended in the vastness of space. Picture all that you cherish and hold dear residing on this blue orb. Reflect on the profound interconnectedness we share with this planet, even from a material standpoint. We know that Earth is intricately linked to the sun, moon, and the rest of the solar system, gracefully orbiting and traversing its path through the cosmos through gravitational energy; they orbit each other while travelling independently. They do not collide with one another; they simply continue to travel on their journeys.

The speed at which the earth travels around the sun is more than 67,000 miles per hour (107,000 kilometres per hour) while spinning on its axis at a rate of 1,000 miles per hour (1,600 kilometres per hour).[3]

---

[3]   Elizabeth Howell and Doris Elin Urrutia, 'How Fast Is Earth Moving?,' Space.com, January 21, 2022, https://www.space.com/33527-how-fast-is-earth-moving.html.

Yet we are so in tune with the Earth's vibration and momentum that this goes unnoticed, and we don't fall off. We are utterly oblivious to the incredible speed at which we travel through the solar system. This demonstrates our physical oneness with our planet and is just one dimension of our connectedness with the Universe and each other.

The word 'Universe' comes from the Latin word 'universum', which translates into 'to be turned into unity' or 'to be turned into a single whole'. This leads us to the first of our Universal Laws, the Law of Divine Oneness. This law is the foundation on which all other Universal Laws are based. It helps us to understand and make sense of the other eleven laws. The Law of Divine Oneness informs us that we are part of a collective consciousness connected to the 'source' or 'God' if that is what you prefer.

It emphasises our interconnectedness with one another and with the divine energy, elevating our understanding of karma to a profound level. In essence, when we extend kindness, we uplift not only others but ourselves as well. The truth that 'I am you, and you are me' resonates deeply within this law, reinforcing our existence's interconnectedness and unity.

Spiritual growth is vital for all of us. As we learn, we develop and grow, and as we learn, develop and grow, we understand the impact vibrational frequency has on the collective consciousness. We are divinely inseparable; everything on this earth plane and cosmos that has ever existed and currently exists is connected. The world does not consist of separate things; the mind is not separate from matter, nor are human beings separate from each other or the world around us, including animals or other living and non-living things.

Freke and Gandy present the words of Hermes Trismegistus in their book *The Hermetica: The Lost Wisdom of Pharaohs*.[4] Hermes was an ancient legendary figure who authored seven Hermetic

---

[4]   Timothy Freke and Peter Gandy, *The Hermetica: The Lost Wisdom of the Pharaohs* (New York, NY: TarcherPerigee, 2008).

principles known as the Hermetic Corpus, or Hermetica. Trismegistus proffered, 'You think that things are many when you view them as separate, but when you see they all hang from the One and flow from the One, you realise they are united, linked together and connected by a chain of being, from the highest to the lowest.'

THE RIPPLE EFFECT

'It is often the small steps, not the giant leaps,
that bring about the most change.'
—HRH Queen Elizabeth II

There is a great power and combined energy in the collective consciousness because it encourages us all to raise our frequency, or vibrational energy, positively through expressing love, gratitude, selflessness, and joy, which positively affects others. Conversely, suppose you venture into the world in a bad mood, feeling sad, angry, fearful, or anxious. In that case, your vibrations are lowered, negatively impacting those around you through what is commonly known as 'the ripple effect'.

Imagine, for a minute, a colleague at work is struggling to meet a deadline. They are stressed and anxious about their current situation because they know the boss will be furious. You come along, aware of the Law of Divine Oneness, and offer them support, a helping hand, and some kind, supportive words. Together, you meet the deadline and submit the work; you are now going home to your families or loved ones at a reasonable hour.

You feel fabulous because *you* did a good deed! Your colleague is so grateful for your help that you go home smiling and feeling good about yourself. Your colleague also goes home feeling good, less stressed and much happier.

Consider the ripple effect: your colleague is in such a good mood now that they have completed their work. They arrive home in the evening and see their elderly neighbour struggling, so he offers to help. The poor man is angry and frustrated with himself because he is having difficulty getting his dustbin down the drive for the sanitation workers the next day. The elderly gentleman is grateful for the assistance, and they both return to their own houses.

Again, consider the ripple effect: the elderly gentleman sits down with his cup of tea and decides to telephone an old friend he hasn't spoken to in a while, just to say 'Hello!' I know I am labouring the point here, but stick with me, none of this would have happened without you, and the support you gave your colleague, *and* without you understanding the Law of Divine Oneness none of this would have happened. I know that you wouldn't necessarily be aware of the effect that you had had on others, but why take the chance?

Cast your mind back to when Caroline Flack's sudden death was announced in 2020. A few days before her death, she reportedly wrote on social media, 'In a world where you can be anything, BE KIND', a quote attributed to the author Jennifer Dukes Lee. If you remember, for quite some time after Caroline's death, #BeKind was trending everywhere. Some people even got the words 'Be Kind' tattooed on their bodies, demonstrating their strength of feeling at that time.

The Law of Divine Oneness helps us calculate and create our reality, which resonates widely throughout our collective consciousness. Within all of us, there is a soul that shines brightly. There is source energy, a divine light that radiates from deep inside each of us *despite* everything we have ever done, how we have lived our lives, or what or who we believe in. Source energy is what binds us together, making us One with each other as well as with the Universe.

IMPRESSION OF INCREASE

*'Know what sparks the light in you. Then use
that light to illuminate the world.'*
—Oprah Winfrey

How we treat others is how we treat ourselves, 'Thou shalt love thy neighbour, as thyself' (Matthew 22:37–39, KJV). We should all aim to operate at a higher frequency, irrespective of who or what we encounter, and we should all have more compassion and care for each other. Self-awareness is critical here. When I studied for my master's degree in healthcare leadership, we were encouraged to consider, 'What is it like being on the receiving end of me?' This has remained with me ever since, and I remind myself of this with every new encounter I have with someone. It has almost become my internal mantra, and I try to ensure that the person I have engaged with leaves with a positive impression of me and who I am.

Proctor refers to this as an 'Impression of Increase', whereby you leave people with an increase after meeting you.[5] What I am trying to say here is we should be aware of how our behaviour, what we say, and how we say it impacts others.

You directly influence the collective vibrational frequency through the ripple effect by operating at a higher vibrational frequency from a feeling of love, peace, harmony, and joy.

---

[5]   Sandy Gallagher, 'What Is the Impression of Increase?,' Proctor Gallagher, December 4, 2021, https://www.proctorgallagherinstitute.com/40274/what-is-the-impression-of-increase.

SPIRITUAL HEALING

*'Once you start replacing negative thoughts with
positive ones, you'll start having positive results.'*
—Willie Nelson

Over the decades, many people have researched how we can use our minds for the greater good to overcome illness and disease. Note here that the word 'disease' comes from 'dis-ease', whereby we are not at ease with ourselves or our bodies. Dr Joe Dispenza spoke about the ability we all have to heal ourselves using our minds.[6] Many hypnotherapists concur with Dr Dispenza, such as Dolores Cannon, the founder of the quantum healing hypnosis technique (QHHT), which centres around using our minds to heal ourselves through accessing what she called the subconscious or higher self to achieve great healing for the body, through hypnosis.[7] Marisa Peer's approach uses rapid transformational therapy (RTT), which also focuses on using hypnosis to gain healing for the body and the mind.[8]

So, if we can heal ourselves, either physically, mentally, or emotionally, using our minds, and as we now understand 'I am you and you are me', then surely it would follow that I can help heal you, too? We can heal each other by fostering and sending more love, compassion, unity, and light to one another and using well-established techniques such as meditation, positive affirmations, journaling, and practising gratitude. Furthermore,

---

[6] Dr Joe Dispenza, Your brain and the immune system, March 12, 2021, https://drjoedispenza.com/dr-joes-blog/your-brain-and-the-immune-system.

[7] 'About Dolores & QHHT®,' QHHT Official Website, March 24, 2024, https://www.qhhtofficial.com/about-us/.

[8] 'RTT Rapid Transformational Therapy: Marisa Peer Method Hypnotherapy,' Rapid Transformational Therapy: RTT®, January 9, 2024, https://rtt.com/.

if we can do that for each other, perhaps we can help heal the earth. How amazing would that be?

In this chapter, we have discussed how being aware of yourself and how you are connected to all that is living now and has in the past can impact you and others through the ripple effect. Now, is your pen poised? It's time to reflect on how you live by this law and what you can do better for your future life to help manifest a happier, more abundant, and prosperous life, whatever that looks like for you. Take the time to do the following exercise.

WOURNAL #1

LIVING BY THE LAW OF DIVINE ONENESS

*'I'd rather regret the things I've done than
regret the things I haven't done.'*
—Lucille Ball

On a scale of 1 to 10, what is your current understanding of this law? (circle one)

No understanding 1 2 3 4 5 6 7 8 9 10 Fully aware of this law

Describe the 'AS IS' picture of your current way of life in line with this law.

____

____

____

____

What can you do better to live by this law? For example, show compassion and be more accepting of others.

____

____

____

____

Why should you embrace this law? What would impact your life the most?

____

____

____

____

When can you demonstrate your use of this law in your daily life? At home, at work, or socially?

____

____

____

Who will benefit when you embrace this law within your life? Family, Friends, Strangers?

____

____

____

Where in your life can you incorporate this law? Where in your life can you demonstrate this law? Think about leading by example.

____

____

____

How will you incorporate this law into your life more effectively

____

____

____

____

CHAPTER 2

UNIVERSAL LAW #2: LAW OF VIBRATION

'We can't help everyone, but everyone can help someone.'
—Ronald Reagan

The Law of Vibration is the primary law; the Law of Attraction starts from this law and is secondary to it. Yet, so many people have focused on attracting what they desire without first checking in with their vibrational frequency or aligning with the Law of Vibration.

This law declares that everything in the Universe, from the smallest atom to the most fantastic galaxies, vibrates, resonates, and moves; nothing ever rests. Even if they appear motionless to the naked eye, they vibrate at energetic frequencies we cannot detect. From solid rock to flowing water, they all have their distinct frequency of vibrating. In essence, everything is energy. Energy functions on frequencies; a frequency is a vibrational level, and there are an infinite number of frequencies. Remember this as we dive deeper into this fascinating law and all the other laws.

EVERYTHING IS ENERGY

'Expect and accept miracles. They are the norm.'
—Mynoo Mayel

Albert Einstein stated, 'Everything is energy, and that's all there is to it. Match the frequency of the reality you want, and you cannot help but get that reality. It can be no other way. This is not philosophy; this is physics.' Proctor, a master in the Law of Vibration, put this more simply: 'You have to become aware that you can, and will, attract anything you require, to cause the picture you hold in your mind to come into form, and this is no accident.' He continues, 'It's all about awareness; there is a marvellous inner world that exists within all of us, and the revelation of such a world enables us to do, attain, and achieve anything we desire within the bounds or limits of nature.'[9]

Humans are complex beings. We vibrate on a frequency unique to each individual. We are primarily made up of energy manifesting in a different vibrational state. All of our thoughts vibrate and emit a frequency. Each thought you send out to the Universe has a frequency. Proctor taught us that the Law of Vibration starts within our minds, creating thoughts that activate the brain cells and impact the Universe.[10] Thought waves transcend all of space and time.

This law is profound; it has significant implications for our modern lives and can impact our health, relationships, and personal development—the higher and greater your vibrational frequency, the greater the potential for personal growth and

---

[9] 'How to Understanding Frequencies, Vibration, and the Law of Attraction with Bob Proctor,' YouTube, May 29, 2023, https://www.youtube.com/watch?v=IVJpEkbf8zc.

[10] 'How to Understanding Frequencies, Vibration, and the Law of Attraction with Bob Proctor,' YouTube, May 29, 2023, https://www.youtube.com/watch?v=IVJpEkbf8zc.

self-realisation. We become conscious creators of our realities through intentionally cultivating positive thoughts and emotions that emit to the Universe and have a high vibrational match for the things we want to attract into our lives.

THE RIPPLE EFFECT ON VIBRATIONS

*'You are only limited by weakness of attention
and poverty of imagination.'*
—Neville Goddard

Think back to the example I gave earlier. Imagine now that you hadn't offered help to your struggling colleague; you saw them stressed and anxious but decided to do nothing. You leave work at 5:30 p.m., leaving your colleague at their desk to continue struggling with their work, and off you go without a care in the world. Your colleague works until midnight and feels dreadful, doesn't eat or drink all evening, but gets the paper finished and on the boss's desk just in time.

As they arrive home, they find their elderly neighbour lying on the ground next to the bin. He'd fallen while struggling to get the dustbin out for the next day. Your colleague phones for an ambulance, and the paramedics take the elderly gentleman away in the ambulance to the accident and emergency department at the local hospital.

The next day, your colleague phones in sick, and the boss is furious about their absence and the standard of the paper your colleague has produced. You get called into the office, and now you get it in the neck. Guess what? You are asked to re-write the paper by the end of the day. This now means you are forced to decline the invitation for Friday night after-work drinks with your mates. It's funny how karma works, but more about that later. If only you could rewind the clock and play this out differently, eh? Sorry, sweet cheeks, it doesn't work like that. I appreciate that this is a bit extreme, and you would never attribute your behaviour to any of the events that followed. Of course, you couldn't foresee what would happen, but as I said before, why take the chance?

So, through the ripple effect, your vibrations are low; as a result, they have affected others around you and attracted more low vibrational situations to you. Yet, in the example I described earlier in the book, the vibrations you were emitting then were high and resulted in a much better experience for all involved.

HOW WORRY AFFECTS VIBRATIONS

'To believe in the things you can see and touch is no belief at all, but to believe in the unseen is a triumph and a blessing.'
—Abraham Lincoln

Now, let's be honest: having high vibrations and positive thoughts at all times is nigh impossible. Research done by the National Science Foundation in 2005 found that the average person had between 12,000 and 60,000 thoughts per day.[11] Furthermore, 80 per cent of those thousands of thoughts were negative, and a staggering 95 per cent of our thoughts are repetitive. No wonder we are so exhausted by the end of the day!

Another study conducted in 2005 by Leahy at Weill-Cornell University Medical College found that 85 per cent of what we worry about never happens.[12] Of the 15 per cent that did, 79 per cent of those involved in the study stated that either they could handle the difficulty better than expected or that it was a source

---

[11] '60,000 or 6,000 Thoughts A Day,' Ciarán Dalton Psychology, LLC., February 23, 2022, https://www.cdaltonpsychology.com/blogrunning-thoughts/60000-or-6000-thoughts-a-day.

[12] Robert L. Leahy, *The Worry Cure: Seven Steps to Stop Worry from Stopping You* (New York: Harmony Books, 2005).

of learning. They concluded that 97 per cent of our worries are baseless and result from an unfounded pessimistic perception.

The worries that consume our minds are a significant source of stress and tension, which can cause exhaustion of the mind and physical body. This shows how much of our internal dialogue is plain old rubbish and does not serve us well. In fact, not only does it not serve us well, but it also causes disease within our bodies and our minds.

We all have ups and downs when things aren't going according to plan, so I am not suggesting that living by this law is easy for one minute. However, I suggest being mindful of your thoughts and feelings. Try to catch the negative ones early and learn how to switch them out for more positive ones; try singing a song, walking, hugging a loved one, or eating chocolate. Have you ever tried hugging a tree? Do whatever works for you and helps you to positively raise your vibration and the vibration of those around you.

This chapter taught us that our thoughts and feelings impact our vibrational frequency and those around us. While keeping track of our thoughts is difficult, we can address the negative ones using the tools featured throughout this book.

WOURNAL #2

LIVING BY THE LAW OF VIBRATION

'There is always light, if only we're brave enough
to see it. If only we're brave enough to be it.'
—Amanda Gorman

On a scale of 1 to 10, what is your current understanding of this law? (circle one)

No understanding 1 2 3 4 5 6 7 8 9 10 Fully aware of this law

Describe the 'AS IS' picture and your current way of life that is in line with this law.

____

____

____

____

What can you do better to live by this law?

____

____

____

____

Why should you embrace this law? What benefits would that bring to your daily life? Can you demonstrate your use of this law in your daily life? At work? At home? In the local pub?

____

____

____

____

When can you demonstrate your use of this law in your daily life? At home, at work, or socially?

____

____

____

Who will benefit when you embrace this law within your life? Family, friends, strangers, colleagues?

____

____

____

Where in your life can you incorporate this law? Where in your life can you demonstrate this law? Think about leading by example.

____

____

____

How will you incorporate this law more effectively into your life? How can you increase your awareness of your vibrational frequency?

____

____

____

CHAPTER 3

UNIVERSAL LAW #3: LAW OF CORRESPONDENCE

'Once you face your fear, nothing is ever as hard as you think.'
—Olivia Newton-John

Have you ever noticed how everything just falls into place some days, and yet other days, what could go wrong does go wrong? Imagine this scenario for a minute; I am sure we have all had days like this. The alarm clock doesn't go off, you shoot out of bed at the time you should be leaving for work, you frantically run around like a headless chicken trying to get dressed, you drop your toothpaste down your top, you can't find your purse, and finally you miss the bus, making you even later for work. Great; what a day you're having, and it's not even 8 a.m.! This is the Law of Correspondence at play: what is going on in your internal world is mirrored by your external world, the basis of this law is 'as within, so without'.

This principle is written in an ancient aphorism, 'as above, so below', which is accredited to the mystical writings of Hermes Trismegistus.[13] The Corpus Hermeticum, where this is written,

---

[13]   Hermès et al., *Corpus Hermeticum* (Paris: Société d'édition 'Les Belles lettres,' 1945).

contains a wealth of knowledge on various philosophical and metaphysical subjects, including the concept of the Law of Correspondence. The principles were of great importance and interest to those intrigued by the relationship between the macrocosm (Universe) and the microcosm (individual).

Hermes believed in a direct link between the two, where the patterns and principles observed in the Universe are also reflected in individual beings and their life experiences. This idea aligns with the concept of the Law of Divine Oneness, suggesting there are underlying similarities and relationships between the cosmos and the intricacies of our lives.

RAISE YOUR AWARENESS

'Life is either a daring adventure or nothing at all.'
—Helen Keller

The Law of Correspondence encourages us to view ourselves and our experiences from a broader perspective. Understanding the fundamental principles governing the Universe can lead us to insights into the nature of our reality and our role in creating it.

The key to living by this law is to raise your awareness, be aware of your inner state of mind, and transform your negative mindset into a positive one as soon as you recognise the negativity you are in, and then sit back and watch how your life aligns with your desired reality.

While writing this book, I discovered the mirror principle. This principle relates to the Law of Correspondence, which states that you must change internally before your external reality can change.

MIRROR OF REALITY

'With the new day comes new strength and new thoughts.'
—Eleanor Roosevelt

The mirror of reality reflects two things: first, your relationship with the world around you and, second, your relationship with yourself. What you see in the mirror is a projection of how you see yourself and the world around you. A way of genuinely harnessing this concept is to write a journal daily about your thoughts or beliefs. This will help to bring those negative thoughts and beliefs to the forefront of your mind so you can consciously deal with them.

If you continue to tell yourself things like 'I'm not good enough' or 'I'm not worthy enough', the mirror will reflect that to you by responding with proof of *why* you're not good enough or worthy enough. If you're going to lie to yourself about 'not being worthy', tell yourself a better lie and stop the mirror from sending you that proof. More on that later!

TAKE CONTROL OF YOUR MIND

'Re-examine all you have been told.
Dismiss what hurts your soul.'
—Watt Whitman

Another favourite of mine is Marisa Peer. She talks about how you must take control of your mind. In one of her presentations, and she has many on YouTube, she hilariously describes how the mind works.[14] Imagine you are asked to do a presentation to

---

[14] 'I Will Teach You How to Destroy Your Negative Thoughts & Feelings Today': Marisa Peer,' YouTube, January 25, 2021, https://youtu.be/4ku0R6ZW0NM?si=R0pDxEDPkp9buNdy.

1500 people, and although you agree, you don't want to do it. So, the dialogue you now have going on in your mind is about how you would do or give anything not to present to 1500 people. Because it wants to please you, your mind says, 'Oh, you don't want to give that presentation. You would give anything not to give a presentation; well, how about a severe bout of explosive diarrhoea instead?'

Whenever I see that video, it makes me laugh out loud because it is so true. The moral of that tale is to be careful about what you tell your mind because it wants to protect you, keep you safe and away from pain, and so it will come up with weird and wonderful ways to steer you away from any perceived harm or threat. In this example, your internal world is genuinely reflected in your outer world, no pun is intended!

Instead of wasting your energy on negativity, create positive affirmations for yourself and about yourself. Regularly repeat them until they are ingrained in your mind. Using the same example above, instead of being fearful of giving the presentation, remind yourself of the times you have presented and with great success, or, if you haven't presented before and the internal dialogue is one of 'I can't do that', then tell yourself 'I haven't done that yet'. Reframe the narrative from a negative to a positive. Just because you haven't done something before doesn't mean you are incapable of doing it; remind yourself that you are a powerful human being and you *can* do anything. Remember, we are the creators of our lives, and we are all magnificent.

WOURNAL #3

LIVING BY THE LAW OF CORRESPONDENCE

'The people who are crazy enough to think they can change the world are the ones who do.'
—Steve Jobs

On a scale of 1 to 10, what is your current understanding of this law? (circle one)

No understanding 1 2 3 4 5 6 7 8 9 10 Fully aware of this law

Describe the 'AS IS' picture and your current way of life that aligns with this law.

____

____

____

____

What can you do to live by this law better? Be more compassionate, caring, and loving to others.

____

____

____

____

Why should you embrace this law? What benefits would that bring to your daily life? Can you demonstrate using this law daily, at home, at work, or socially?

____

____

____

____

When can you demonstrate your use of this law in your daily life? At home, at work, or socially?

____

____

____

Who will benefit when you embrace this law in your life? Family, friends, strangers, colleagues?

____

____

____

Where in your life can you incorporate this law? Where in your life can you demonstrate this law? Think about leading by example.

____

____

____

How will you incorporate this law more effectively into your life? How can you increase your awareness of your vibrational frequency?

____

____

____

CHAPTER 4

UNIVERSAL LAW #4:
LAW OF ATTRACTION

'You do not find the happy life. You make it.'
—Camilla Eyring Kimball

So here we are; we have finally arrived at the Law of Attraction, the most famous law of them all, and one that most of us have heard of, thanks to Rhonda Byrne and *The Secret,* but what exactly is it? And how can we apply this law to our own lives? We have already established that this law is secondary to the Law of Vibration and decrees that 'like attracts like'.

Manifestation is a result of the Law of Attraction. By that, I mean you manifest things into your life through attraction, but to attract the things you want, you must first be on the correct vibrational frequency to the things you want in your life, which is why this law is the secondary law to the Law of Vibration.

Let's dive deeper into this and unpack it together!

Dolores Cannon stated that as infinite divine beings, we can have anything we want; we just need to ask.[15] Unfortunately, as we enter these bodies, which we call our own, we have

---

[15] 'QHHT {Quantum Healing Hypnosis Technique} Official Training,' QHHT Official Website, July 1, 2024, http://QHHTofficial.com/.

forgotten about our origins and that we are primarily spiritual beings having a human experience. We have come to Earth to manipulate energy. Dolores meant that we are here to create, and the Universe's job is to give us anything we want; the only limits to this are those we put on ourselves with our self-limiting beliefs or our unconscious self-sabotage. Dolores said, 'We don't believe that we are primarily spiritual beings, and we doubt the power each of us has.'

It's as simple as placing an order at McDonald's. You place your order and wait for delivery, but when ordering from the Universe, you must be specific about what you want. At McDonalds, you wouldn't order a double cheeseburger when you really wanted a fillet-o-fish. It's the same with your order to the Universe. If you want a fillet-o-fish, then place the order for that and not a double cheeseburger. Do you get where I am coming from here?

Dolores advises us that there are only two rules we must obey when placing our orders with the Universe;

1. Never create anything that will harm another person.
2. Never create anything that will take away from another person.

Bear these in mind, and the world is your lobster … or is it oyster? I never can remember! Speaking of deep-sea creatures, let's go even deeper now and reflect on your school days when you learnt about magnets and how they work. Ready?

MAGNETISM AND THE LAW OF ATTRACTION

*'You will face many defeats in life, but
never let yourself be defeated.'*
—Maya Angelou

The Law of Attraction is described as a magnet, but this goes beyond only attracting material things. This law is reflective of our body's electromagnetic field. But what does this mean?

Let's consider, for a second, how a real magnet works. The National Geographic Society explains magnetism as the force exerted by magnets when they attract or repel each other.[16] The motion of electric charges causes magnetism. Every substance is made up of tiny units (Atoms). Each atom has electron particles that carry electrical charges. The electrons spin and circle the atom's core (nucleus), and this movement generates the electrical current, causing each electron to act like a magnet. Some substances cancel out the magnetism because the equal numbers of electrons spin in opposite directions. Materials such as cloth or paper are examples of this. However, in metals such as iron, most of the electrons spin in the same direction, causing the atoms in the metal to become magnetic, but they are not magnets. All magnets have north and south poles; opposite poles attract each other, while the same poles repel each other. When you run a piece of iron along a magnet, the atoms of the north-seeking poles align in the same direction as each other, creating a magnetic field; the piece of iron has become magnetic, but once you remove the piece of iron from the magnet, the magnetic field is broken, and the iron returns once again to being just a piece of iron.

---

[16] 'National Geographic Society,' Education, accessed July 31, 2024, https://education.nationalgeographic.org/.

Great! I hear you say, but what does that have to do with the Law of Attraction? I'm getting to it. Hang in there.

So, now consider that your body is also a magnet. The Chakras—of which there are seven—are spinning wheels of energy running through the centre of the body, symbolising the energy within and creating an electromagnetic force. Our body's electromagnetic nature creates a rotating vortex emanating from all sides. The Chakras act like magnets, attracting and pulling energy into themselves.

The mind and body equal the north pole, known as the highest Chakra or the crown Chakra. The south pole is the lowest Chakra, or the root Chakra, at the base of the spine. Your state of mind determines the energy that flows through these chakras. Positive thoughts keep the energy flowing, maximising the effect of the electromagnetic force flowing through the body.

POSITIVE THINKING AND THE LAW OF ATTRACTION

'Love the life you live. Live the life you love.'
—Bob Marley

The effect of positive thinking has been thoroughly researched over decades, and it has been established that positive thinking produces happy hormones, such as serotonin and dopamine. Negative thoughts, however, have the opposite effect and cause a biochemical imbalance, which disrupts the flow of energy and releases stress hormones such as adrenaline and cortisol into our systems. The research I mentioned earlier, in the Law of Vibration chapter, concluded that ninety-seven per cent of our negative thoughts and worries were foundationless and only serve to cause turmoil in our minds and our physical bodies. This release of stress hormones into our bodies is what they were referring to.

Proctor spoke about how our subconscious minds will only accept thoughts that are a match to our emotional state.[17] Therefore, you must create the right emotional state when reprogramming your mind. The subconscious mind is receptive when you have feelings of harmony, gratitude, love and joy. At this time, the subconscious mind is malleable to your desires. Conversely, when you are in fear or feeling stressed, your body releases increased levels of stress hormones, the hormones involved in our fight-or-flight response. These chemicals will not allow adequate access to your subconscious mind.

Be aware of your feelings because this is an indicator of your vibration. Thoughts provide an electrical charge, whereas feelings provide a magnetic charge. Together, they create your electromagnetic field, determining what you attract into your life.

Consistently living in a heightened emotional state of peace, serenity, love, and harmony—regardless of your external circumstances—will ensure you are on the right frequency of your desired things. You cannot help but attract them. Furthermore, as a result of this positive state of mind, you will experience more joy and happiness as the Law of Attraction comes into play, attracting like-to-like.

---

[17]   'Tell Us What You Want, We'll Show You How to Get It,' Proctor Gallagher, July 18, 2024, http://www.proctorgallagherinstitute.com/.

HOW WE UNCONSCIOUSLY BROADCAST OUR EMOTIONS

'We cannot solve our problems with the same thinking we used when we created them. Match the frequency of the reality you want, and you cannot help but get that reality.'
—Albert Einstein

Let us consider that the heart and emotions are intrinsically linked. The heart symbolises love, and love is the most powerful emotion regarding attraction. According to the HeartMath Institute, the magnetic field produced by the heart is one hundred times greater than that of the brain, and it can be detected several feet away from the body in all directions.[18] Simply put, we are broadcasting our emotions without even realising it.

It is suggested that heightened emotions of the heart produce a coherence of brainwave patterns and prime your brain to create your ideal future. The greater this coherence, the more potent the energy is, and the more powerful your thought waves generate time and space. As we know, there may be a time delay, but eventually, it will come.

Attraction refers to the things you want in your life that are in harmony with your dominant thoughts. Vibration correlates with tuning into the frequency of those things and staying there until you get them. As we have established, everything is frequency, and frequency equals a vibration level. The brain is an electronic switching station which functions on frequencies, and there are an infinite number of frequencies.[19]

---

[18] 'Mysteries of the Heart,' HeartMath Institute, accessed July 31, 2024, https://www.heartmath.org/resources/infographic/mysteries-of-the-heart/.

[19] 'Tell Us What You Want, We'll Show You How to Get It,' Proctor Gallagher, July 18, 2024, http://www.proctorgallagherinstitute.com/.

The life you desire is in your imagination but on a higher frequency than the one you are in now. The Law of Attraction requires you to imagine and see the good in your desire in vivid detail. The Law of Vibration requires you to hold onto that frequency by maintaining the picture in your imagination and feeling the excitement of having what you desire, accepting and knowing that the good you seek is coming. These two laws work together in unison; you cannot have one without the other.

Do not let your current circumstances dictate your frequency. Use your conscious mind to impress your desires onto your subconscious mind. Through repetitive exercises, such as visualisations and affirmations, your body's frequency will change, which compels the subconscious mind to move you towards taking action to get the desired result. Boom! Doesn't that sound amazing?

So, if you believe your situation is hopeless, the only things that will show up for you are inaction, demotivation, unhappiness and frustration. Conversely, if you think your dream is unfolding, that higher vibration will drive you to act inspired. It is the vibration that causes you to act and the action that sets up the attraction.[20]

Proctor stated that someone who has a low frequency will have a low income, whereas someone on a high frequency will benefit from a high income. It is our birthright to live a life that we truly desire, and it's our choice to go out and get it. There's one thing for sure, though: it ain't coming if you spend all your time watching television, scrolling through Instagram or doing other mundane habitual stuff, *that* isn't working towards your goal.

Consider this as a process:

- Everything starts with a thought.
- Thought drives a desire.

---

[20] 'Tell Us What You Want, We'll Show You How to Get It,' Proctor Gallagher, July 18, 2024, http://www.proctorgallagherinstitute.com/.

- Desire changes the vibration.
- Vibration changes action.
- Action sets up an attraction.
- Attraction determines results.

Andrew Carnegie was one of the wealthiest men in the USA in the 1900s. He said, 'Any idea that is held in the mind, that is emphasised, that is either feared or revered, will begin at once to clothe itself in the most convenient and appropriate form available.' Put simply, what you hold in your mind, be that something you want or don't want, will always show up whether you want it to or not.

So many people think about what they don't want in life, 'I don't want this job', 'I don't want this relationship', 'I don't want to struggle for money all the time.' Well, as we know, that's precisely what you will get more of! So, choose to think positively about what you *want* to happen or show up in your life, and *do not* focus on what you *don't* want to happen. Get your mind onto a higher frequency that is aligned with your burning desire.

WOURNAL #4

LIVING BY THE LAW OF ATTRACTION

'There is nothing impossible to him who will try.'
—Alexander the Great

On a scale of 1 to 10, what is your current understanding of this law? (circle one)

No understanding 1 2 3 4 5 6 7 8 9 10 Fully aware of this law

Describe the 'AS IS' picture of the current way of life in line with this law.

____

____

____

____

What can you do to live by this law better? Be more compassionate, caring, and loving to others.

____

____

____

____

Why should you embrace this law? What benefits would that bring to your life?

____

____

____

____

When can you demonstrate your use of this law in your daily life? At home, at work, or socially?

____

____

____

____

Who will benefit when you embrace this law in your life? Family, Friends, Strangers?

____

____

____

____

Where in your life can you incorporate this law? Where in your life can you demonstrate this law? Think about leading by example.

____

____

____

____

How will you incorporate this law into your life more effectively?

____

____

____

____

CHAPTER 5

UNIVERSAL LAW #5: LAW OF INSPIRED ACTION

*'Success is only meaningful and enjoyable
if it feels like your own.'*
—Michelle Obama

So you're probably asking, 'What does "inspired action" mean?' Well, let me explain: inspired action differs from regular task-based action because when your action is inspired, you are in tune with your intuition and feelings. When you are doing something to achieve your goal, it brings you joy, excitement, and motivation. It is driven by passion and a burning desire to succeed in whichever area of your life you wish to gain success in.

For example, Thomas Edison dreamed of inventing an electric lamp. Although he failed thousands of times, he stood by his dream until it became a physical reality.[21] Edison did not sit back and wait for the invention to manifest into reality; he worked tirelessly to *make* it happen. With steely determination,

---

[21] Napoleon Hill, *Think and Grow Rich: Original 1937 Edition* (Duke Classics, 2012).

he took inspired action and never gave up. Imagine what life would be like for us if he had!

The greatest inventors of our time started with a dream, a thought, or an inspiration, which they all acted upon with tenacity and perseverance, an unwavering belief, and a burning desire to achieve something extraordinary. This isn't something that *just* happened by chance or luck. It happened because these historically great men and women *made* it happen.

The Law of Inspired Action teaches us that when we take inspired action toward our dreams, the Universe responds by providing us with resources, opportunities, and intuition to help us achieve our goals. It states that to achieve your dreams, you must first take action. It's not enough to dream and hope your life will change; you must take inspired action.

Most of us are guilty of waiting for the 'right time' to start things. 'When the kids start school', 'When I have enough money', or 'When I have less stress at work' … sound familiar? This is a destructive merry-go-round that we must get off to move forward and achieve what we want in our lives.

Remember the Law of Divine Oneness? It states that we are all connected, and the Universe responds to our thoughts and *actions*. When we take *inspired action,* we send a strong message to the Universe that we are serious about achieving our goals. As we have already established, the Universe responds by sending us opportunities and resources to help us achieve what we want.

To make this law work for you, you must be clear about your goals. Secondly, you must listen to your intuition, that gut feeling, and those nagging thoughts demanding your attention, and watch for the opportunities that come knocking; these are all ways the Universe is trying to communicate with you.

All ideas and thoughts first start with a dream. However, dreaming alone is not enough; it requires inspired action and motivation to realise your desires. Imagine you had an intuitive feeling about buying a lottery ticket but ignored it. You wouldn't sit there watching the national lottery draw on a Saturday evening expecting to have your numbers drawn out and discover you were a millionaire, would you? Now, that would be a miracle!

LISTEN TO YOUR INNER GUIDANCE

'If you cannot do great things, do small things in a great way.'
—Napoleon Hill

The smallest of steps can result in the most significant progress, and although they may be scary, you must take the first step. 'Those who are afraid of new ideas are doomed from the start.'[22] Your first steps don't need to be perfect, grandiose, or elaborate, and you don't need to be able to see the whole picture. You just need to be consistent in your approach, which will impact your momentum, and soon enough, you will have made progress.

Fear is the biggest disabler of our time; it grinds us all to a halt and must be overcome. It often presents itself through procrastination. What is this fear all about? Fear of failure? Fear of success? Fear of ridicule? Fear of what others will think of us? These unfounded fears are obstacles in the way of us taking inspired action, and they zap our motivational energy. Think about reframing your fears into more positive thoughts and affirmations. What are your negative beliefs about yourself (self-limiting beliefs)? These are usually fears wrapped up with a different label.

Challenge those beliefs of not being good, worthy, or deserving. Question where these beliefs have come from and

---

[22]   Napoleon Hill, *Think and Grow Rich: Original 1937 Edition* (Duke Classics, 2012).

address them head-on.[23] Focus on your strengths and the possibilities your dreams, goals, and a new way of life will bring. Allow your imagination to play in your mind. Now, what do these pictures look like? Better than those negative thoughts of fear, doubt, and impossibilities?

Take time to engage with your inner voice and intuition, sit quietly for a while, and notice what your intuition is trying to tell you. Listen to your inner guidance and what actions feel right to you. Don't dismiss any ideas or thoughts that come up. You may think the inspiration is too challenging and will stretch your limits. Moving out of your comfort zone will bring you closer to your dreams and the life you desire, so embrace it with bravery and gratitude and let it guide you to your highest potential. The Universe will not guide you towards something you cannot manage. Everybody has the resources inside them to be successful.

What stirs up your curiosity? Pay attention to it. Spend time researching and exploring new ideas and see where they take you. Most importantly, raise your awareness of the signs, symbols, and synchronicities the Universe is sending you. Dolores Cannon teaches us that there are no such things as coincidences. It is the Universe responding and guiding you, so allow it to do what it naturally wants to do.

---

[23]   'I Will Teach You How to Destroy Your Negative Thoughts & Feelings Today': Marisa Peer,' YouTube, January 25, 2021, https://youtu. be/4ku0R6ZW0NM?si=R0pDxEDPkp9buNdy.

HOW DOES IT MAKE YOU FEEL?

*'Be so happy that when other people look
at you, they become happy too.'*
—Anonymous

If you are unsure whether something is an inspired action, try a small experiment and ask yourself what feelings this conjures up inside you? What does this scenario tell you? Is it sparking joy deep within you? Is it bringing excitement? If so, the likelihood is that this is inspired action.

Let me share with you some of my journey concerning inspired action. In 1992, I decided I wanted to be a physiotherapist. Nothing too grandiose there, you might think. Well, I had left high school pregnant with no qualifications. Many had predicted that I wouldn't amount to anything. Don't ask me where this ambition of being a physiotherapist emerged from because I have no idea. I just knew that I wanted to prove those doubters wrong, and I wanted to make my mum proud again. Back then, I felt that I had let her down. As an adult, I know now that this wasn't the case, but let's be realistic: your sixteen-year-old daughter having a baby is not what any parent would want for their child!

Another motivator I had at the time was that I wanted to provide well for my son and give him all the opportunities he wanted to pursue. I didn't understand what being a physiotherapist entailed; all I knew was that I wanted to help and serve people in a healthcare setting, and I knew I didn't want to be a nurse. I also knew this would be a massive challenge, but I was prepared to face it head-on.

I decided to do some research, so pre-internet days, I arrived at the job centre to enquire about the qualifications needed to achieve my goal. I was met by a lady sitting behind a desk who smirked and remarked, 'What makes you think you can be a physiotherapist?' as she directed me to the corner of the room by pointing her finger towards the section where I could find the required information. This wouldn't be the last time I would be laughed at or discouraged from my desire to succeed, and by a stranger, too!

I noted what qualifications I would need and set a strategy for myself. I didn't know what I was doing back then, but after reflecting on it numerous times, I realised this was my first goal-setting attempt. I had a clear vision, and it would take me seven years to achieve it! As my son started school at age five, I, too, returned to full-time education, embarking on two GCSEs in the first year of my studies and three GCSEs the following year.

During this time, I was informed of an access course I could apply for at a university approximately fifty miles from where I lived. This would give me the equivalent of two A levels, meaning I could reduce my seven-year plan to six. I was successful with this course, so I applied for a Bachelor of Science Degree in Physiotherapy at the same university, and despite coming up against some obstacles during the interview process, I successfully gained a place on the course. It was 1995, and I graduated as a physiotherapist three years later. My son was almost eleven years old.

THE IMPACT OF INSPIRED ACTION

'Ever tried. Ever failed. No matter.
Try again. Fail again. Fail better.'
—Samuel Beckett

The purpose of telling you this part of my story is to demonstrate how taking inspired action has impacted my life. No amount of wishful thinking or the use of the Law of Attraction would ever get me to the goal of becoming a physiotherapist. However, using the other Universal Laws, I achieved my goal, even though I didn't know about them then. I was not discouraged by people trying to criticise, give 'advice' or tell me I couldn't achieve my dream. I was determined and took inspired action to gain a better life for my son and me, and that's precisely what we got.

The lesson I have since learnt from my experience of becoming a mum at sixteen years old is that we all have choices and options. If we want to make something of our lives and be successful, we must choose to do something about it and essentially decide to create a different reality for ourselves.

If what you wish to do is right and you believe in it, then go ahead and do it![24] Don't wait to unlock your success. Start small, but act now.

In this chapter, we have uncovered how taking inspired action to attain your goals and dreams is paramount to your success. Let's now look at how intentionally embracing this law can impact your life and bring you more fulfilment.

---

[24] Napoleon Hill, *Think and Grow Rich: Original 1937 Edition* (Duke Classics, 2012).

WOURNAL #5

LIVING BY THE LAW OF INSPIRED ACTION

'It's no use going back to yesterday because
I was a different person then.'
—Lewis Carroll

On a scale of 1 to 10, what is your current understanding of this law? (circle one)

No understanding 1 2 3 4 5 6 7 8 9 10 Fully aware of this law

Describe the 'AS IS' picture of your current way of life in line with this law.

____

____

____

____

What can you do better to live by this law? What is motivating you? What is inspiring you to take action?

____

____

____

____

Why should you embrace this law? What benefits would that bring to your life?

____

____

____

____

When can you demonstrate your use of this law in your daily life? At home, at work, or socially?

Who will benefit when you embrace this law in your life? Family, Friends, Strangers?

Where in your life can you incorporate this law? Where in your life can you demonstrate this law? Think about leading by example.

How will you incorporate this law into your life more effectively?

CHAPTER 6

UNIVERSAL LAW #6: LAW OF PERPETUAL TRANSMUTATION OF ENERGY

'Attitude is the 'little' thing that makes a big difference.'
—Sir Winston Churchill

This law states that all energy can be transmuted into different forms, that *change* is a constant within the Universe, and that energy is constantly moving. *Nothing* ever stays the same. This also relates to the energy within each of us because this, too, is continually moving, transforming, or transmuting, and we can use this to our benefit.

Perpetual means constant, and transmutation means transformation. Therefore, this law relates to a continuous transformation of energy. What it's teaching us is that we can all transform (or transmute) the power within us to change our realities. If you master this law, you can manifest anything you wish. However, manifestation isn't just about an abundance of money or a big posh house and a fast car; it can also relate to an abundance of love, health, relationships or joy. It is for *you* to choose what you want an abundance of.

AS ABOVE SO BELOW

'I alone cannot change the world, but I can cast a stone across the waters to create many ripples.'
—Mother Theresa

Practically, to embrace this law, you can take the happiness you feel about something or a situation and harness it through a visualisation exercise or journaling. Equally, if you are feeling low, you can transform your energy into something better by consciously switching your thoughts. Try thinking about a good night out with your friends or a joke someone told you, and hold on to the happiness this evokes within you. Try the visualisation exercise or journaling from *that* new place of joy, or if you're so inclined, you can channel your newfound energy into an exercise session at your local gym! This will further compound your higher vibrational state by releasing your happy hormones.

A hermetic principle explains the relationship between the Law of Perpetual Transmutation of Energy and the Law of Vibrations: 'As above so below, as within so without, and as the Universe so the soul.' This principle suggests a relationship between your vibration and your energy. Once this is fully understood, it becomes easier to allow higher-vibrational energy to flow through you, which creates a shift in your reality.

TWO CONSTANTS IN THE UNIVERSE

'Life is really simple, but we insist on making it complicated.'
—Confucius

There are only two constants in the Universe: one is of energy, and the other is of matter; neither can be created nor destroyed; they can only ever change form. Think about water; for instance, in a solid form, it is ice; in a liquid form, it is water; and in a gaseous form, it is steam. You can apply a physical element to ice, such as heat, which *will* change its form. However, it will always be water.

This means all energy transmits into and out of form and can never be stopped. Everything in the Universe is a constant motion of energy. By harnessing this concept, you can tap into it and transform it into *anything* you desire.

ADOPT A GROWTH MINDSET

'You have brains in your head. You have feet in your shoes.
You can steer yourself any direction you choose.'
—Dr Suess

We all have the power to change the conditions of our lives through our consciousness, to simply and successfully manifest the desires we hold in our minds into physical products. Adopting a growth mindset will enable you to believe in yourself and your ability to shift your negative thoughts into more positive ones. Therefore, according to Hermetic principles, you must cease to live in a negative emotional state, such as fear, shame, guilt, or apathy, as this state does not serve you well on many levels.

By harnessing higher vibrations, we can transform our lower vibrational states, and through doing so, we will transform our lives for the better. We must be mindful of our negative emotions and learn to process them efficiently and effectively through perpetually transforming our energy, which aligns with what this law teaches us. Emotions are 'energy in motion', and if we fail to process our negative emotions fully, they can be stored within the body, causing us stress, depression and anxiety in the future.

Raise your vibration by expanding your consciousness through the Universal Laws, which will help you embrace courage, willingness, reason, and acceptance. In this state of mind, energy flows freely from one form to another; we must learn to adopt a non-resistant approach to change and become a vessel for the perpetual transmutation of energy.

This chapter has demonstrated to us the importance of changing our vibrational energy from a negative to a positive and how this can be achieved through our minds and our thoughts, compounded further through small actions. Let's look at how we can accomplish this with the next wournal.

WOURNAL #6

LIVING BY THE LAW OF PERPETUAL TRANSMUTATION OF ENERGY

*'The glow of one warm thought is to
me worth more than money.'*
—Thomas Jefferson

On a scale of 1 to 10, what is your current understanding of this law? (circle one)

No understanding 1 2 3 4 5 6 7 8 9 10 Fully aware of this law

Describe the 'AS IS' picture and current way of life in line with this law.

____

____

____

____

What can you do to live by this law better? Be more compassionate, caring, and loving to others.

____

____

____

____

Why should you embrace this law? What benefits would that bring to your life?

____

____

____

____

When can you demonstrate your use of this law in your daily life? At home, at work, or socially?

____

____

____

____

Who will benefit when you embrace this law in your life? Family, Friends, Strangers?

____

____

____

____

Where in your life can you incorporate this law? Where in your life can you demonstrate this law? Think about leading by example.

____

____

____

____

How will you incorporate this law into your life more effectively?

____

____

____

____

CHAPTER 7

UNIVERSAL LAW #7: LAW OF CAUSE AND EFFECT

*'Opportunity is missed by most people because it
is dressed in overalls and looks like work.'*
—Thomas Edison

This law is closely associated with the principle of Karma. However, the Law of Cause and Effect goes much further. In essence, this law states that for every effect, there is a cause and vice versa; there are no accidents or coincidences, and every effect has a specific and predictable cause. Likewise, every cause has a specific and predictable effect. A famous quote from the renowned essayist, poet, and philosopher Ralph Waldo Emerson stated, 'The Law of Cause and Effect is the law of laws. It is the law of the natural world and the law of the spiritual world. It is the law that governs all things, and it is the law that determines the course of our lives.'

Newton's third law is the Law of Cause and Effect, but it is reframed. Remember Newton's third law? He stated that for every action, there is an equal and opposite reaction. Consider what happens if you were to throw a ball against a wall. The wall will return the ball with equal force and velocity along the same arc. Throw the same ball hard and fast against the wall, and it will return to you equally hard and fast. Do the opposite, and the opposite will happen. In other words, little actions will produce little effects; significant actions will produce substantial effects. Bear this in mind when you reflect on your goals and how you will achieve them.

DISEMPOWERING VS EMPOWERING

'The only impossible journey is the one you never begin.'
—Tony Robbins

Focusing on effect is disempowering for humans because the effect is based on the past—and the past no longer exists. These are only memories of our past experiences that impact the way we feel. We must train our minds to focus on the cause, where we are empowered and can create a different internal and external world. This is a much more powerful standpoint, where you can consciously create your environment through your thoughts and emotions.

Another way of thinking about this law is 'you reap what you sow'. If you sow specific seeds, you will get specific outcomes. This may appear harsh at first, but the truth is that your current circumstances directly result from the seeds you have sown in the past. Your current life *represents* all the decisions and actions you have taken up to the present day. Consider the house you live in, the car you drive, or your job. These are all past decisions and actions that have contributed to the creation of the reality you are experiencing right now.

A powerful question to ask yourself when viewing your current environment is, 'How did I create this for myself?' Identifying the steps you took to get where you are now will raise your awareness and assist you in making better life choices along the way. Presuming that you are unfulfilled in some way with your current reality, that is!

IMPACT OF CAUSE AND EFFECT ON OUR LIVES

'Life itself is the most wonderful fairy tale.'
—Hans Christian Anderson

Consider this: causes are the beliefs, decisions, and actions—whilst effects are the results, situations, and circumstances. So, for example, imagine you are in financial debt. This is the effect of living beyond your means and spending too much money (cause). Or it could be that you're overweight (effect) because you eat unhealthily and don't exercise (cause). Are you with me so far? On a positive note, you may be in a perfect financial position (effect), and this is because you save a percentage of your salary (cause), or it could be that you're at your ideal weight, wearing your favourite jeans (effect) because you have made healthy choices and exercised daily (cause).

However, the cause alone does not generate an optimal effect. For this to happen, we need to factor in conditions, but a condition alone will not cause an optimal result. The equation we need to consider here is Cause + Condition = Optimal Effects. Imagine that you are overweight and you can't fit into those gorgeous jeans you spent a fortune on; if you continue in the same vein—eating an unhealthy diet and not exercising—your reality won't change. However, changing the condition by applying a healthy diet and exercise regime will achieve optimal effects. I don't know about you, but that was a real epiphany!

RIPPLE EFFECT OF CAUSE AND EFFECT

'Go confidently in the direction of your dreams!
Live the life you've imagined.'
—Henry David Thoreau

The concept of this law promotes that your conscious actions are not isolated events; they initiate a chain of reactions and have a ripple effect throughout the collective consciousness.[25] This means that we should all be aware and mindful of our actions. For example, showing someone kindness (cause) might make someone's day (effect). The opposite result would happen if you spoke to someone too harshly, but remember that our words stay with someone long after we say them.

Ancient philosophical practices such as Buddhism and Hinduism teach us that whoever sends a thought or action into the Universe will receive its consequences, or its effect, in one form or another. Furthermore, they also state that you cannot avoid the consequences of your actions in time. That's great if the outcomes are positive but less so if they are negative.

Let me reassure you here: if you consider yourself to be, on the whole, a good and kind person, and you do something that causes harm or hurt to another, inadvertently and unintentionally, the consequences for this harm or hurt would not be as significant as they would be if you had deliberately set out to cause damage to someone else. Therefore, it is the intention behind the action that matters most.

This law advocates that nothing is down to luck; there is only an action that returns to its source through an effect. All actions have consequences, and these consequences, good or bad,

---

25   Wise Minds, "WARNING: These 12 Universal Laws Will Change Your Life Forever," YouTube, June 15, 2024, https://youtu. be/r-3aWDSRKPE?si=4RFv90TOsVTjFFys.

will cause a positive or negative chain of reaction for yourself or others around you.

The key to living by this law is to create positivity, and a pleasant chain of reactions will follow in alignment with it. Live your life by generating good, simple actions, thoughts, and behaviours that will create positive effects.

Again, consider that old-fashioned saying, 'You reap what you sow.' This quote has been with us for centuries, and yet, I suspect, very few of us think about its origin or, indeed, the meaning behind it.

Furthermore, we can view our worlds from a cause-or-effect perspective—we can either take responsibility for our situation or find someone to blame. It is disempowering to us when we blame others, yet empowering when we take responsibility for something that has happened. So, for example, we can say, 'I am late for work because you rang me, which made me late leaving the house, which meant I got caught up in traffic.' Or, we can say, 'I am late for work because *I* took a call from you, which meant I got caught up in traffic.' Can you see the subtle difference here? One is to blame (you) coming from the angle of effect, and one is taking responsibility (I) from the perspective of cause.

This chapter has taught us how we should try to look at things differently. Now, let's examine ways to incorporate this law more deeply into your life and watch how it changes for the better.

WOURNAL #7

LIVING BY THE LAW OF CAUSE AND EFFECT

*'Life is like a bicycle. To keep your
balance, you must keep moving.'*
—**Albert Einstein**

On a scale of 1 to 10, what is your current understanding of this law? (circle one)

No understanding 1 2 3 4 5 6 7 8 9 10 Fully aware of this law

Describe the 'AS IS' picture and current way of life in line with this law.

____

____

____

____

What can you do better to live by this law?

____

____

____

____

Why should you embrace this law? What benefits would that bring to your life?

____

____

____

____

When, in your daily life, can you demonstrate your use of this law? At home, at work, socially?

____

____

____

____

Who will benefit when you embrace this law in your life? Family, Friends, Strangers?

____

____

____

____

Where in your life can you incorporate this law? Where in your life can you demonstrate this law? Think about leading by example.

____

____

____

____

How will you incorporate this law into your life more effectively?

____

____

____

____

CHAPTER 8

UNIVERSAL LAW #8:
LAW OF COMPENSATION

*'You can, you should, and if you're brave
enough to start, you will.'*
—Stephen King

This law states that we will be compensated for our efforts or contributions, no matter how small or grand they may be. The Law of Compensation is closely related to the Law of Cause and Effect because it also advocates that you reap what you sow.

Ralph Waldo Emerson, an influential thinker in 1841, famously wrote, 'A person will be compensated for their efforts and their contribution to society.' Furthermore, Emerson stated, 'When you give to others, you will be compensated in time. There may be a delay, but the compensation will come. However, this may not come back to you as you expect.'

This law does not require relentless work, stress, and toil. It's more about the genuine, authentic effort involving emotional and intellectual efforts, not just the physical effort you can offer.[26]

---

[26]   Wise Minds, "The Law of Compensation Simply Explained (Universal Laws)," YouTube, November 19, 2021, https://youtu.be/ud9NbI7Roa0.

Additionally, to avoid diminishing the effects of this law, I would suggest not to give your time or effort in an obligatory, begrudgingly or resentful way but to give it with love, honour, and respect and for the joy it will bring you, knowing that you have done a good deed for another person, through giving your time and effort so freely. Do not consider what you will get back in return, and have no expectations.

EXPECTATIONS

'What we think and feel deep inside of ourselves
will be reflected back to us in our physical world.
What we believe is what we become.'
—Wallace D. Wattles

Dodson talks about the expectations we have of each other in his series of videos about Being Authentic.[27] The term he uses to observe 'expectations' is 'A Secret Contract'. I will explain it briefly: Dodson states that a secret contract happens when you do something for someone else and expect something in return, but *without* communicating this expectation to the other person, it is an *implied* expectation, which is based in your subconscious and many of us don't realise we are doing it. The example I want to offer here—and one I am sure many of you can relate to—is one of Christmas time; consider this scenario: we buy a friend a gift for Christmas, but there isn't a gift from them in return, resulting in us feeling upset and resentful. We have 'secretly contracted' with our friends and subconsciously expected a gift in return, but *failed* to tell them about our expectations, and now *we* are upset because they didn't buy us a Christmas gift.

---

[27]   Frederick Dodson, 'Being Authentic Part 6: Self Awareness', Reality Creation, August 26, 2023, https://www.realitycreation.org/being-authentic-part-6-self-awareness/.

Considering the Law of Compensation, we should not do things with the mindset that we will get something back in return, nor should we feel compelled to reciprocate if someone does something nice for us. If we want to live authentically, and by the Law of Compensation, we should only do the things we want to do and for the pleasure of doing it. We should put faith in the Universe and know that it will compensate us differently, because that is how the Law of Compensation works.

BALANCE IN THE UNIVERSE

'Many of life's failures are people who did not realise how close they were to success when they gave up.'
—Thomas Edison

The Universe works in mysterious ways. What I mean by that is the Universe has ways of balancing all things out: give positively and receive positive things back to you; give with resentment or negativity, and you will be compensated with such things in return.

Another popular expression you'll be familiar with is, 'One good deed deserves another', which dates back to the 1400s. We may traditionally think of this term as 'If you do something nice for others, and they will do something nice in return', but without any confirmation of what this saying means, I would like to offer a slightly different perspective on it, in line with the universal Law of Compensation. 'You do something nice for someone, and the *Universe* will do something nice for you in return.' I wonder, did those living in the 1400s understand this law better than we do today? Perhaps they did!

RANDOM ACTS OF KINDNESS

*'Keep smiling because life is a beautiful thing,
and there's so much to smile about.'*
—Marilyn Monroe

Random acts of kindness go a long way. I recently heard about an exercise involving random acts of kindness, where small handwritten notes of positivity, compassion, or motivation were given out to strangers—by strangers—just to lift other people's spirits. The results were fascinating, as some of these notes were passed on again and again to other strangers. Remember the ripple effect I mentioned earlier? The recipients of the handwritten notes reported that it felt good for their souls to receive these notes. Without a doubt, this will have increased the recipients' vibrational frequency and that of the people who delivered the notes, too. It is a simple consequence of a few words of love or encouragement shared among strangers, but the impact is immeasurable.

On a more personal level, I have an elderly neighbour whose daughter works tirelessly to take good care of her. Each summer, during the warmer days, I often water her garden while doing my own. I try to do it covertly because I want to avoid any secret contracting. I do it simply because each week after the sanitation workers have emptied the bins, mine miraculously makes its way up my driveway and positions itself outside the side gate of my house … courtesy of my already stretched, busy neighbour's daughter. This is not a secret contract because it brings me pleasure to help my neighbour's daughter and to see her garden flourish with beautiful, colourful flowers, which in turn will bring my housebound neighbour some joy too. Some may downplay this as being neighbourly and nothing special on either of our behalf, but small acts of kindness like this come back to us. To be honest,

I am not even sure she realises that I water her mum's garden, which is just fine with me!

The key to embracing this law is to consistently give more to the world than you receive in return. We can all do more to help ourselves and increase our happiness simultaneously through simple acts such as smiling, laughing, and loving the people around us. My granddaughter laughs at me when we walk the dog together because I will say hello to everyone I walk past. She always says, 'Nanna, why do you speak to everyone?' and I tell her it is because it is nice to be friendly. Consider how you can make others happy, however small that may be. None of us should expect others to make us happy—*we* are responsible for our own happiness—but we can all do small things to help others be happy—even if it's not our responsibility. As the law states, you will be compensated with more happiness in return.

So, let's take some time to look at what you can do to increase your happiness and that of your nearest and dearest with the next wournal.

WOURNAL #8

LIVING BY THE LAW OF COMPENSATION

'It does not matter how slow you go as long as you do not stop.'
—Confucius

On a scale of 1 to 10, what is your current understanding of this law? (circle one)

No understanding 1 2 3 4 5 6 7 8 9 10 Fully aware of this law

Describe the 'AS IS' picture and current way of life in line with this law.

What can you do better to live by this law? Be more compassionate, caring, and loving to others.

Why should you embrace this law? What benefits would that bring to your life?

When can you demonstrate your use of this law in your daily life? At home, at work, or socially?

____

____

____

Who will benefit when you embrace this law in your life? Family, Friends, Strangers?

____

____

____

Where in your life can you incorporate this law? Where in your life can you demonstrate this law? Think about leading by example.

____

____

____

How will you incorporate this law into your life more effectively?

____

____

____

____

CHAPTER 9

UNIVERSAL LAW #9: LAW OF RELATIVITY

'Our greatest weakness lies in giving up. The most certain
way to succeed is always to try just one more time.'
—Thomas Edison

This law states that everything in the Universe is relative. For example, there is no such thing as good or bad, fast or slow—when viewed independently, everything is neutral. However, this changes when you compare a 'thing' with something else. Let me explain: if something is viewed in isolation, it is just how it is. It is the comparison with something else that provides us with perspective. This is a law you will most likely be aware of, as it is evident in our daily lives.

Galileo was an Italian astronomer in the 1600s. He wrote about the principle of relativity and stated, 'It is impossible, by any mechanical means, to say whether something is in motion or at rest.'[28] So, let's consider the following example: two cars travel side by side in the same direction and speed. The passengers in each vehicle are unable to decipher if the car they are in is moving or

---

[28] 'Galileo,' Encyclopædia Britannica, July 29, 2024, https://www.britannica.com/biography/Galileo-Galilei.

76

not, but if one of those passengers takes a fixed reference point—say of a tree alongside the road on which they are travelling—they will be able to say with certainty that the vehicle is moving. In this example, the perspective of motion is only understood when compared with something else, which is static.

Over hundreds of years, human beings have been obsessed with relativity. In fact, we have designed many instruments to measure it; for example, the speedometer (speed), the thermometer (temperature), the odometer (distance) and the barometer (air pressure), all of which were invented to capture the relativity of things in our physical world.

DIFFERING PERSPECTIVES OF REALITY

*'If you want to make your dreams come true,
the first thing you have to do is wake up.'*
—J.M. Power

On a more individual level, we can all look at our world through rose-coloured spectacles, and what we see is not always accurate. That's because we filter our reality by distorting, deleting and generalising everything based on our experiences. If you can, cast your mind back to an argument you have had. The general sequence of any disagreement is as follows: you argue your point from the perspective of your reality—which is based on your filtering system, which is based on your own experiences—the person you are arguing with does the same—based on their experiences and filters—and around the same vicious cycle you both go, over and over, until one of you gives up, or you agree to disagree. It is impossible to get someone else to see your point of view, even more so when emotions are heightened, as we each have different versions of the truth. Whatever 'truth' is!

The Law of Relativity can be used for personal improvement or for your detriment. It asks us to be more mindful of our perspective on everything and accept that multiple perspectives can be applied to any situation or challenge. We each perceive reality in our own unique ways.[29] Remember the old saying, is your glass half empty or half full? This is a perfect example of the Law of Relativity because it depends on your perception of reality and how you view the glass.

If you are an optimistic, positive type of person—a real-life Tigger—then you will consider your glass to be half full; however, if you are pessimistic and negative—and a real-life gloomy Eeyore—then you will view your glass as being half empty. But it doesn't have to be that way; as we know, we can change our viewpoint by changing our perspective and altering our thought patterns.

Everything is relative, so in the grand scheme of things, your problems or challenges are not as bad as you perceive them. *You* are the person who assigns meaning to things, so it is down to you to decide if something is terrible or is, in fact, an opportunity for growth and personal development.

Life is full of challenges, but you are equipped to handle them no matter what they are. You can use challenges as an opportunity to learn lessons, gain experience, and evolve into a more competent version of yourself, or you can allow them to consume you and distract you from how you want your life to be.

---

[29] Wise Minds, "The Law of Relativity (The Spiritual Aspect of Relativity) Explained," YouTube, November 23, 2021, https://youtu. be/xj6KQa9DGM0.

MISUSE OF THE LAW

*'The secret of success is to do the
common thing uncommonly well.'*
—John D. Rockefeller Jr

Misusing this law can impact your self-esteem and momentum towards your goal or desires; it reminds us that all pain and suffering come from wanting something more than we already have. However, it's important to note that a difference exists between wanting and needing something. For example, wanting designer clothes, fast cars, and a palatial pad is not essential for happiness. Savvy marketing strategies planted the desire for these things in our subconscious minds, causing us to compare our material world with others. How often do you buy new shoes, a coat or a car? In the beginning, you love it, it's the best thing ever, you wear it/use it a couple of times, and then all of a sudden, it no longer has the same sparkle or shine it once had, so you move onto the next shiny thing that catches your eye ... no? Hmm, just me, then, who suffers from shiny object syndrome!

Maslow's Hierarchy of Basic Human Needs—depicted as a pyramid—is based on physiological, safety, love and belonging, esteem and self-actualisation. When these are fulfilled, human beings are satisfied. Maslow stated that the items at the pyramid's base must be achieved before we can ascend to the next level. However, more modern thought is that each level overlaps and is, in continual review, dependent on life experiences and challenges. It is not a linear concept, as Maslow indicated, but rather a fluid one that flexes and moves with what life throws our way.

At no time does Maslow say that to be a fulfilled human being, you must have the latest Mulberry handbag or Gucci purse and a red Ferrari! These 'wants' derive from societal pressures, and most of us fall under the spell of aiming for these material things. The main reason we desire these items is to keep up with the Joneses! By having them, we can portray the sort of person everyone else aspires to be, or worse still, we want them so that we can *compete* with others. Misuse of the Law of Relativity involves constantly comparing ourselves with others, whether we do that consciously or otherwise. If you can distinguish between wants and needs, you will separate yourself from unnecessary desires and take back your power.

STOP BEING ENVIOUS OF OTHERS

'Everything you can imagine is real.'
—Pablo Picasso

This constant comparison of yourself with others, who you *presume* are doing better in life than you, will trigger associated negative feelings and emotions. These feelings can be viewed at opposite ends of a spectrum, one supremely positive and the other profoundly negative. Let's look at this in greater detail. The internal dialogue associated with this positive or negative perspective is critical. If the chatter in your head includes thoughts of anger, resentment, or jealousy towards another person for the things they have or achievements they have made, the emotions that arise within you *will* be negative. Remember that everything starts with a thought—you think a thought, and your feelings are generated—this impacts the vibrational state you emit to the Universe and the actions you may take. These negative thoughts can drive inertia, ultimately moving you further away from attaining your goals. This negativity can also result in feeling miserable, irritable, and wretched, and you may feel you have no hope for your future.

At the opposite end of the spectrum, where you have a more positive perspective of someone more successful, wealthier, or has more material things than you. Your thoughts about this are positive in nature, where instead of comparing yourself and being envious of them, you feel genuine joy and happiness for that person and all that they have. If your thoughts are more in line with them deserving it all—because they have worked so hard for it—and your feelings are of excitement, empowerment, or joy, this can compel and drive you to take inspired action.

A slight tweak in our perspective can enormously impact our lives, and positive thoughts and feelings can cause us to take positive action toward our goals. If we allow it, these things can inspire and drive us towards a commitment to our cause, and if someone else can achieve these things, then there is no reason you can't achieve them, too.

Ultimately, you are not competing against another person, so you cannot lose. By all means, you can use what they have as inspiration to get what you want in life. Remember, we all start at the base of a steep mountain, but instead of channelling envy and resentment at those on the summit, channel this energy and move along the same path they took to get there. To improve and develop yourself, trust a proven system, a blueprint someone else has successfully developed and used.

IMPACT OF MISUSING THIS LAW

'There are no secrets to success. It is the result of preparation, hard work, and learning from failure.'
—Colin Powell

Emotion is energy in motion. Your use of the Law of Relativity determines if this energy is progressive or regressive. Dr Maxwell Maltz, an American plastic surgeon, authored numerous books about Psycho-cybernetics, a system of ideas that he claimed could improve one's self-image, leading to a more prosperous and fulfilling life. Maltz stated, 'You can never outperform your self-image.'[30] If you misuse the Law of Relativity, you will continue to reduce your self-image. Reducing your self-image reduces the results you will get. However, it's not all doom and gloom; if you improve your self-image, the results you get will improve in line with this.

Taking action in the present time changes your self-image. What Maltz suggests is to first expand your self-image from within so that you can express it from without. Remember the Law of Correspondence? 'As within, so without.' Before long, you will bond with the idea of an expanded self-image and be able to talk the talk *and* walk the walk!

Let us reflect on goals for a moment. We must consider two types of goals in line with this law: high-order goals and low-order goals. High-order goals are those you are deeply passionate about and are driven to achieve. On the other hand, low-order goals are those based on a competitive nature and are purely developed to compete with others. Competition is a misuse of the Law of Relativity. Do you need a 5000 sq foot property on the Malibu beachfront or that red Ferrari car capable of breaking the sound barrier? Or is this desire a direct result of a misuse of the law? Often, friends aspire to have specific things and adopt the same wants and goals just to look comparatively well. This is the most destructive way you can break the rules of this law. This attitude will only generate stress, unhappiness, frustration, and probably a vast amount of debt as you aim to achieve what they have.

Relativity is helpful as it provides us with a perspective. Be mindful, consider every thought, feeling, and action through the lens of relativity, and do it in a way that empowers you, not in a way that disempowers you.

---

[30] 'Maxwell Maltz', Wikipedia, March 29, 2024, https://en.wikipedia.org/wiki/Maxwell_Maltz.

To fully adopt the Law of Relativity, you need to perform two simultaneous actions; the first is to recognise that everything is an illusion. Thomas J. Stanley wrote a book, *The Millionaire Mind,* in which he writes that the wealthiest of people all drive *used* cars.[31] So, in reality, the many people driving brand new cars on our roads are actively deep in debt and one paycheck away from bankruptcy ... food for thought?

Once you apply the illusory filter to those you deem superior to you in some way, the second thing to consider is the concept of happiness. Psychologists have discovered that everything we do is to gain pleasure and avoid pain. The lesson here is the next time you find yourself undermining your self-worth by misusing the law, stop and think about the truth behind the illusion. Realise that we all have unique gifts and talents that make us better than others in specific arenas. In other words, you do you and do it to the best of your abilities.

This chapter has informed us how the Law of Relativity can positively shape our lives and our happiness *if* we embrace it fully and avoid competing with others. In truth, we *all* have more than others in certain areas of our lives, so be grateful for that and direct your efforts towards your passions. Being the best at everything is impossible, so focus your efforts on *your* strengths, and you will excel further. So, onto the next wournal.

---

[31] Thomas J. Stanley, *The Millionaire Mind* (New York: RosettaBooks, 2010).

WOURNAL #9

LIVING BY THE LAW OF RELATIVITY

*'There are two ways of spreading light: to be the
candle or the mirror that reflects it.'*
—Edith Warton

On a scale of 1 to 10, what is your current understanding of this law? (circle one)

No understanding 1 2 3 4 5 6 7 8 9 10 Fully aware of this law

Describe the 'AS IS' picture and current way of life in line with this law.

____

____

____

____

What can you do to live by this law better? Be more compassionate, caring, and loving to others.

____

____

____

____

Why should you embrace this law? What benefits would that bring to your life?

____

____

____

____

When can you demonstrate your use of this law in your daily life? At home, at work, or socially?

____

____

____

____

Who will benefit when you embrace this law in your life? Family, Friends, Strangers?

____

____

____

____

Where in your life can you incorporate this law? Where in your life can you demonstrate this law? Think about leading by example.

____

____

____

____

How will you incorporate this law into your life more effectively?

____

____

____

____

CHAPTER 10

UNIVERSAL LAW #10: LAW OF POLARITY

'If you can dream it, you can do it.'
—**Walt Disney**

Before approaching the Law of Polarity, I want to tell you about the science behind this law. Our science lessons at school taught us that everything has a positive and negative charge and that all matter is bound in place by a strong nuclear force. We know that every atom has within it a neutron (neutral charge) combined with a proton (positive charge) and an electron (negative charge). The proton and the electron are essential for the cohesion of all matter, as they play a crucial role in binding everything together through the Law of Polarity. This law is often taken for granted, but we wouldn't exist without it.

The Law of Polarity is a law that all of us will be aware of, but probably haven't realised how important it is in our world or our existence, as everything has a polar opposite, or some would say duality. Take, for example, young and old, hot and cold, light and dark, fast and slow, or up and down. Suffice it to say you can't have a positive without a negative. Furthermore, the law states that everything has an equal and opposite, which is necessary for balance within the Universe.

POSITIVE AND NEGATIVE TERMS

'Always remember, your focus determines your reality.'
—George Lucas

The existence of the law of polarity, in terms of positive and negative, decrees that there is more than one way of thinking about things. You can take any situation in life and give it the meaning you want to because you can see it as a negative or a positive experience. So, why do most of us think and focus on only one polarity? Primarily on negativity, when in reality, there is another (positive) pole to consider, which won't zap your vibrational energy.

I appreciate that this law sounds very simplistic, but that's because it is; it's all about choice. We could, if we so choose, focus on the positive side of polarity to move our lives forward and become happier. We can make a decisive shift in our thinking, our feelings, and our actions towards a negative event and choose to shift our reaction to the event to a more favourable positive reaction.

Let me give you an example: You disagree with a colleague one day in the office. Let's say you take the last tea bag out of the canister, and before you can refill it with new tea bags, your colleague confronts you in a less-than-polite manner, calling you selfish and lazy at the top of their voice so that everyone in the office can hear. Consider the Law of Polarity: at one end of the spectrum is kindness (positive), and at the other is unkindness (negative). As a human being, you are faced with two choices: Do you tell your colleague what you think of them and that they are the one person in the office most of your other colleagues don't like?

THERE IS ANOTHER WAY

*'The question isn't who is going to let me;
it's who is going to stop me.'*
—Ayn Rand

You could choose to spew some equally unkind words in their direction in a fit of anger for the way they have just spoken to you—which, let's face it, would probably leave *you* feeling bad for the rest of the day, negatively impacting *your* vibrational energy—or, you could choose the positive, kind approach, apologise politely, fill the canister up with tea bags and walk away calmly, leaving them to continue on their path of destructive nastiness.

Granted, it's a rather absurd example, but I wanted to demonstrate to you that if we can detach ourselves from the way we think, feel, and react to negative situations if we can remain impartial and not get entangled in the craziness of life events, then, we can identify what the negative situation is teaching us and how it is showing to us what we *don't* want in our lives. Equally, focusing on the positive end of the polarity spectrum informs us about what we want *more* of in our lives.

EVERY CLOUD HAS A SILVER LINING

'Courage is grace under pressure.'
—Ernest Hemingway

If something negative happens, there must be something good about it. I am not saying this will be obvious immediately, but it will eventually become clear. Let me share with you for a moment a personal story: my ex-husband decided to end our marriage after just three short years. He was no longer happy, but rather than discuss it with me and try to improve our relationship, he decided to leave for another woman. For a long time, I didn't feel like he had done me a favour as I nursed my broken heart and sank into a pit of despair—sadly, I felt like the bottom had fallen out of my world and that my wounds were irreparable. But, further down the line, I began to understand that it was the best thing he could have done for me.

Since my marriage broke down, I have achieved so much more in my life that, if I'm honest, I probably wouldn't have done if we had stayed together, and to be truthful, so has he. Perhaps this resonates with you? Have you been in a similar situation? Maybe you have since met someone who loves you unconditionally, or you have had more success in your career, or you simply realise how much better off you are financially. Maybe this is where the saying 'every cloud has a silver lining' comes from.

During adverse life events, ask yourself, what is this situation trying to teach me? How can I flip this negative situation into a positive? What action can I take forward to improve myself or my life? I am not saying this will be easy, and it will feel a bit clunky to begin with, but like everything, if you practise, take a step back, and ask yourself some challenging questions, you will develop the skills required to live by the Law of Polarity. Let's take a moment to wournal how you will achieve this.

WOURNAL #10

LIVING BY THE LAW OF POLARITY

'What lies behind you and what lies in front of you
pales in comparison to what lies inside of you.'
—Ralph Waldo Emerson

On a scale of 1 to 10, what is your current understanding of this law? (circle one)

No understanding 1 2 3 4 5 6 7 8 9 10 Fully aware of this law

Describe the 'AS IS' picture and current way of life in line with this law.

____

____

____

____

What can you do to live by this law better? Be more compassionate, caring, and loving to others.

____

____

____

____

Why should you embrace this law? What benefits would that bring to your life?

____

____

____

____

When, in your daily life, can you demonstrate your use of this law? At home, at work, socially?

____

____

____

Who will benefit when you embrace this law in your life? Family, Friends, Strangers?

____

____

____

Where in your life can you incorporate his law? Where in your life can you demonstrate this law? Think about leading by example.

____

____

____

How will you incorporate this law into your life more effectively?

____

____

____

CHAPTER 11

UNIVERSAL LAW #11: LAW OF RHYTHM

'I have learned not to allow rejection to move me.'
—Cicely Tyson

This law is one we see evidence of in our everyday lives. It is not one that we can discount or argue with. Let me explain: the Law of Rhythm states there is a cyclical nature of everything; consider for a minute the low tide follows the high tide, spring follows winter, night follows day, and even our breath can be attributed to this law—as we inhale, so we exhale.

One of the seven Hermetic principles relates to the rhythm of life, or Law of Rhythm, as discussed in the Kybalion, a study of the Hermetic principles based on the philosophy and teachings of the ancient Greeks and Egyptians, written in 1908 and attributed to William Walker Atkinson.[32] The Kybalion states, 'Everything flows out and in; all things rise and fall; the pendulum swing manifests in everything; the swing to the right is the measure of the swing to the left; rhythm compensates.'

---

[32] 'William Walker Atkinson,' Wikipedia, November 23, 2023, https://en.wikipedia.org/wiki/William_Walker_Atkinson.

NATURAL CYCLES AND EQUILIBRIUM

*'Things work out best for those who make
the best of how things work out.'*
—John Wooden

The Law of Rhythm decrees that everything flows in natural cycles and that nature must maintain an equilibrium by fine-tuning all its moving parts. This law is closely related to the Law of Cause and Effect because there is always a reaction to every action. In line with this, consider the law of perpetual transmutation that teaches us that change is constant, and as we know, energy is perpetual. If we apply the Law of Rhythm to our everyday lives, we can console ourselves during difficult times and believe that better times must be on the way.

We can't always stay on a high, and we can't always stay low. We will always experience ups and downs, highs and lows. Still, suppose you can establish the viewpoint that everything happens for a reason and accept that the lows are not permanent and that they, too, will pass. In that case, you will build personal resilience and strength of character as these lows are sent to challenge us and provide us with life lessons.

Remember, Earth is a school; we are here to experience life in all its glory.

LIFE LESSONS

'Take up one idea. Make that one idea your life -- think of it, dream of it, live on that idea. Let the brain, muscles, nerves, and every part of your body be full of that idea, and just leave every other idea alone. This is the way to success..'
—Swami Vivekananda

Everything you go through in life prepares you, teaches you, and develops you to become a more competent, resilient person, ultimately a better version of yourself. Circumstances can influence your feelings—if you let them—as a human, you have the right to choose. It is, therefore, your right to decide how you want to react to adverse situations. You can fight against it, slump into a pit of despair and sadness, causing suffering to you and those around you, or you can accept it, go with the flow and choose to look at the bigger picture. You can choose not to struggle or suffer by putting your difficulties into perspective and riding the wave until better times come your way once again, and they will, if the Law of Rhythm is anything to go by!

Suppose you allow negative thoughts and feelings to linger, and you do nothing but focus on how tough life is for you, for example, how wronged you were by your ex or boss, you are administering negative energy to the problem, which only prolongs the pain and suffering. Your outer world is a reflection of your inner thoughts and feelings. Therefore, battling against the outside situation is futile if you maintain its cause on the inside. On the other hand, you can decide not to give it much thought and energy and trust that it will soon pass by. The key here is understanding what the situation is trying to teach you. There are no coincidences, so the problem must teach you a lesson.

YOU GET TO CHOOSE

'Learn from yesterday, live for today, hope for tomorrow.
The important thing is not to stop questioning.'
—Albert Einstein

Remember that your present circumstance is not your fate. By altering your mindset, you can positively affect the outcome. The way I see it is during difficult times, you have three options: you can choose to give up, you can continue on your journey, or you can adapt. If you choose to give up, then you will never achieve your goal, and you will never see what you are *truly* capable of.

Secondly, you can persist with your plans. Still, if you are expending a lot of energy on your goal and not seeing much in return, you may start to doubt your abilities and whether your plan will ever come to fruition. Remember that you must reap what you sow. You cannot reap and sow in the same season. You must allow the Universe to respond during the gestation period. Hill stated that 'Persistence is to the character of man as carbon is to steel.'[33] Focus on your goal, and the Universe must give way to your desires. There is no other way!

Finally, you can adapt, while persistence and sheer determination are admirable. Still, again, if you are expending a lot of energy and the results you are seeing are not commensurate with this, and your time frames have lapsed, maybe you are not on the right path, and the goal you have set is not in line with your highest good, or your soul contract. Are you familiar with the saying, 'What is for you won't pass you by?' Don't struggle or stress; swim with the tide and not against it; reevaluate your plans and perhaps your goal, and if you are meant for something, it will come.

---

[33] Napoleon Hill, *Think and Grow Rich: Original 1937 Edition* (Duke Classics, 2012).

The Law of Rhythm teaches us to accept all phases of our lives with a new perspective and ride the waves, as this is all part of life's journey and rich tapestry. We are spiritual beings having a human experience, and the Law of Rhythm ensures that we receive a diverse spectrum of what life has to offer us. Time to think about how you can bring this Law into your life effectively so that you start to feel more fulfilled.

WOURNAL #11

LIVING BY THE LAW OF RHYTHM

*'All you need is the plan, the road map, and the
courage to press on to your destination.'*
—Earl Nightingale

On a scale of 1 to 10, what is your current understanding of this law? (circle one)

No understanding 1 2 3 4 5 6 7 8 9 10 Fully aware of this law

Describe the 'AS IS' picture and current way of life in line with this law.

____

____

____

____

What can you do to live by this law better? Be more compassionate, caring, and loving to others.

____

____

____

____

Why should you embrace this law? What benefits would that bring to your life?

____

____

____

____

When, in your daily life, can you demonstrate your use of this law? At home, at work, socially?

Who will benefit when you embrace this law in your life? Family, Friends, Strangers?

Where in your life can you incorporate this law? Where in your life can you demonstrate this law? Think about leading by example.

How will you incorporate this law into your life more effectively?

CHAPTER 12

UNIVERSAL LAW #12: LAW OF GENDER

'Champions keep playing until they get it right.'
—Billie Jean King

So, here we are at the last of our twelve Universal Laws, the Law of Gender. This law is one of the lesser-known laws, and contrary to what you might think, it is not about the gender—or sex—you were born into or identify as. This law relates to the masculine and feminine energies within us—and within everything—and is similar to the Law of Polarity, as this law also focuses on the opposite ends of a scale.

The Law of Genders states that everything possesses masculine and feminine energies, represented by the yin and yang. Each energy has unique characteristics that are essential for a balanced life. Masculine energy is driven, action-oriented, and goal-oriented, while feminine energy is intuitive, compassionate, and nurturing. We must maintain harmony between these energies to live a fulfilled life. Overemphasising one over the other can lead to imbalances and negative consequences. Striking a balance between masculine and feminine energies is vital to achieving happiness and well-being.

THE DOMINANCE OF MASCULINE ENERGY

*'Someone is sitting in the shade today because
someone planted a tree a long time ago.'*
—Warren Buffett

We live in a world where masculine energy dominates. We are raised from an early age and programmed to take the initiative, be driven and ambitious, persistent and relentless, and goal-oriented. Both males and females draw on this energy and use these characteristics for business, work and life goals. The world around us dictates that we must overemphasise our masculine energy to succeed. However, there must be a balance to this, so it is imperative to our well-being that we maintain a work-life balance, and this is where our feminine energy steps in.[34]

Feminine energy presents itself through intuition and compassion, empathy and nurturing, transparency, accountability, and communication. This type of energy is very giving, receptive and passive. If feminine energy is dominant, intuition will result in wise choices, and emotional intelligence will provide excellent interpersonal skills and an innate ability to manage and resolve conflicts.

---

[34] Wise Minds, "The Law of Gender Explained (What Is The Law Of Gender)," YouTube, December 5, 2021, https://youtu.be/Oo0jYxh5ka8?si=6TWv9E9WWhnss1JL.

EMBRACE BOTH ASPECTS

'Once you choose hope, anything's possible.'
—Christopher Reeve

If we lean more towards one energy than the other, we create an imbalance that could manifest in undesirable ways. Too much masculine energy may mean difficulty switching off after work. You won't appreciate the importance of downtime and won't factor in enough time for rest and recovery. Those with a strong dominance toward masculine energy will tend towards perfectionism and may have difficulty with interpersonal relationships, whereby work is the priority, and the risk of burnout is high.

The Law of Gender is a crucial concept to understand. If you find yourself leaning too much towards feminine energy, you may struggle with motivation, indecisiveness, and an inability to separate yourself from others' emotions. This can lead to prioritising others' needs over your own and neglecting self-care in the process. You should tap into your feminine energy when feeling disconnected, unfulfilled, or overly self-critical to bring balance to your life.

On the other hand, embracing masculine energy can help you focus on achieving your life-changing goals. However, when faced with significant decisions, utilising your feminine energy may be more beneficial. It's essential to recognise that both energies are necessary for success, regardless of gender. You can effectively harness their power by being aware of and acknowledging the presence of these energies in your life.

FINDING YOUR BALANCE

*'It is not the strongest of the species that survive,
nor the most intelligent, but the one most responsive to change.'*
—Charles Darwin

Like the Law of Polarity, there isn't a specific formula for utilising the Law of Gender. It's about recognising when each energy is needed and how they complement each other. Whether conceiving an idea (feminine energy) or strategising to bring that idea to life (masculine energy), both are essential for growth and development. Striking a balance between these energies is critical to achieving success and fulfilment in all areas of life.

You must use both energies to be successful, and everyone can express one or the other, irrespective of what sex you are. To grow and develop, we must understand the importance of both these energies and their roles in the world. This chapter has explained how we must embrace both masculine and feminine energies to maintain harmony and balance in our lives, and we must remember that one is not superior to the other.

WOURNAL #12

LIVING BY THE LAW OF GENDERS

'Whatever you think the world is withholding from
you, you are withholding from the world.'
—Eckhart Tolle

On a scale of 1 to 10, what is your current understanding of this law? (circle one)

No understanding 1 2 3 4 5 6 7 8 9 10 Fully aware of this law

Describe the 'AS IS' picture and current way of life in line with this law. Are you more dominant in one gender than the other?

____

____

____

____

What can you do better to live by this law? Think about the decisions or goals you have. Which gender is best to use when tackling these issues?

____

____

____

____

Why should you embrace this law? What benefits would that bring to your life?

____

____

____

____

Will your approach towards others be different now you know about this law?

____

____

____

When can you demonstrate your use of this law in your daily life? At home, at work, socially? Can you think of examples when you should draw on one gender more than the other?

____

____

____

Who will benefit when you embrace this law in your life? Family, Friends, Strangers? What is the benefit of the benefit?

____

____

____

How will you incorporate this law into your life more effectively? Consider the next time you are faced with something—like a life event—which gender will you choose to allow to dominate? Which one would you usually have allowed to dominate?

____

____

____

____

Let's consistently remind ourselves of the Universal Laws, which are the laws of behaviour. If we embrace these laws in our lives and change our behaviours in response to our new learning, then we can truly transform our lives for the benefit of humankind.

Now that we have dipped our toes into the Universal Laws and considered their impact on our manifestation abilities, we should look at what's on offer in our toolkit. The first one we will look at is goal setting. So, let's jump straight in!

SECTION TWO

THE TOOLKIT

*'You define your own life. Don't let
other people write your script.'*
—Oprah Winfrey

CHAPTER 13

THE TOOLKIT

'Change the way you look at things,
and the things you look at change.'
—Wayne Dyer

Welcome to the toolkit! In the coming pages, we will look at the tools I have selected for the toolkit, which you can work through at your own pace. Remember to wournal your way through it to gain the best results in your life!

Now, let's get started. In 1989, Locke and Latham published *A Theory of Goal Setting and Task Performance*. Their work identified why goal setting was important and what factors influenced people's efforts when achieving goals.

- Goals narrow attention and direct efforts to goal-*relevant* activities, moving them away from perceived undesirable and goal-*irrelevant* actions.
- Goals can lead to more effort.
- Goals influence persistence.

Factors that influence goal-directed efforts include:

- Goal difficulty: the level of perceived difficulty in achieving the goal.
- Goal commitment: the extent to which the person is interested in reaching the goal.
- Goal specificity: the clarity one has around what is required or needed to achieve the goal.

Working for many years as a physiotherapist in stroke rehabilitation, I understand the power of goal setting. When a stroke survivor arrived on the unit for the first time, I would assess their physical abilities and ascertain what functional ability they would need before they were eligible to be discharged home. It was at this time we would set their goals. For example, a patient may need to be able to mobilise ten metres, with a walking stick, unaided, within one month to independently access their toilet at home. This goal would focus on what we aimed for within the next month, informing my treatment plan.

As a physiotherapist, I used the SMART goal-setting model, which we will discuss later. Patients often needed to catch up on how far they had come, so this tool was an excellent way of demonstrating their progress at our goal review meetings.

In the arena of this book, goal setting is simply writing down what you desire or want to achieve in your life. Do you want to be slimmer, wealthier, healthier, in a more loving relationship, more successful in your career, or even write a book? Goals can focus on anything—personal desires and academic or professional goals. Research conducted by Dr Gail Matthews from the Dominican University in California concluded that 33 per cent of us are more likely to achieve our goals if we write them down than those who don't.[35]

Furthermore, Matthews' research demonstrated that setting goals is not quite as simple as writing them down and leaving them alone month in and month out. Goal setting requires a commitment to regular review and accountability from your peers. Good intentions will *not* achieve the results you are looking for.

So, first, you need to establish what you want to achieve. What is your goal? What is your desire? The Universe doesn't comprehend size, so I advise thinking big, exciting, empowering, and unlimited. Imagine a fantasy life and have an enormous vision for your future!

SET SPECIFIC GOALS

'If your dreams don't scare you, they are too small.'
—Richard Branson

Hill wrote that all those who historically accumulated great fortunes first did a certain amount of dreaming, wishing, hoping, and desiring before they achieved their goals.[36] He said every great leader was a dreamer from the dawn of civilisation to the present day. Now, granted, this statement was made in 1937, but it is as relevant today as it was back then. You only need to look around at those who have had great success in *our* lifetimes. People like Duncan Bannatyne and Richard Branson, for example. Both of

---

[35] Gail Matthews, "The Impact of Commitment, Accountability and Written Goals on Goal Achievement," Dominican University of California, 2007, https://scholar.dominican.edu/cgi/viewcontent.cgi?article=1002&context=psychology-faculty-conference-presentations.

[36] Napoleon Hill, *Think and Grow Rich: Original 1937 Edition* (Duke Classics, 2012).

these men left school with little education or qualifications, and in Branson's case, he struggled throughout his formative years with dyslexia. Despite this, both have achieved great success and are multi-millionaires. They had a dream, a goal, and a burning desire to win the game of life.

Many people feel adrift in life, with no real focus on where they are heading or why. Personal goal setting is fundamental to achieving success. You wouldn't get into a car to go somewhere for the first time without planning how you will get there, how long the journey will be, and what route you will take. So why do so many of us sleepwalk through life without a plan? Or at least some idea of where we are heading? In Lewis Carroll's book *Alice's Adventures in Wonderland*, Alice talks to the Cheshire Cat and says, 'If you don't know where you're going, any road will take you there.' How true this statement is, albeit in a fictional book.

Let me tell you, the most successful people in this world have goals. They know exactly where they are heading. They may not have all the answers for how to get there, and they may need to enlist others' help to work out the finer details, but they *will* have a vision and a plan, and so can you, right?

Setting one to three goals demonstrates a commitment and sends a positive message to the Universe that you value yourself. By that, I mean you are investing in your personal growth and development. As well as setting these goals, choose one gigantic goal, one that will stretch, challenge, and expand you. Our souls love to grow and develop, and goal setting is a tool to enable this expansion.[37]

Goals need to be specific; there is no wishy-washy stuff here. This is serious! When goals are specific, we convince ourselves that we are getting there ... wherever 'there' is. If goals aren't specific, then we struggle to savour our achievements. We have

---

[37]   'Frederick Dodson—Success Coach,' Reality Creation, accessed June 17, 2024, https://www.realitycreation.org/.

no benchmark from which to work or the ability to assess how far we have come through our efforts, and, therefore, we can easily dismiss the progress we have made.

GROWING IN YOUR GOALS

'Two most important days in your life: the day you were born, and the day you discover why.'
—Mark Twain

All too often, people set unachievable goals, which causes them to feel disempowered, disappointed, and bad for their self-perceived failings. So, let's put this into perspective: you wouldn't set yourself a goal to run a marathon and only allow yourself three weeks of training to achieve it, would you? Now, that would be madness! Unless you are Mo Farah, I suspect it would be completely unachievable, and you would be setting yourself up to 'fail'. That said, one of Aristotle's famous quotes was, 'No great mind has ever existed, without a touch of madness'. Hmmm! I will let you ponder on that one.

In terms of perceived failings, my advice is to see any failures for what they are, which is a temporary setback and an opportunity to grow, learn, and develop. There is no such thing as failure, only feedback.

If you are struggling, ask yourself, 'Is my mind having difficulty believing I can achieve such great things? Do I still have self-limiting beliefs that need addressing?' Perhaps your goals need a rewrite? Despite all of this, what you don't want to do is give up. An old proverb is 'Fortune always helps the brave' (P. Terentius 161 BC), meaning that those who take risks are richly rewarded, so bear this in mind before you throw the towel in.

Furthermore, Hill wrote, 'No more effort is required to aim high in life, to demand abundance and prosperity than is required to accept misery and poverty.'[38] Therefore, think beyond your current reality and allow yourself to dream and visualise your new life.

Now, on the flip side of 'failures', make sure to celebrate and savour all of your successes with positive affirmations. Give yourself a pep talk about how fantastic you are for getting this far and not giving up when times are difficult. Remind yourself how worthy you are of this achievement and how you deserve success. However small the achievement, it doesn't matter; your mind doesn't comprehend size, and neither does the Universe.

SHARE YOUR GOALS

'In a battle between logic and emotion, emotion always wins.'
—Marisa Peer

Some have suggested that sharing your goals adds more power to them. It communicates your intention to the Universe and others, which helps you stay committed to them. If you are happy to share your goals with others, try setting yourself a goal review meeting with people you trust, those who will lovingly champion you and help you celebrate your success. This is when you can discuss and chart your progress, and the group can compassionately hold you accountable, ensuring that you stay focused on your accomplishments and the next milestone.

On the contrary, Hill suggests that if others' opinions or criticisms easily sway you, then it may be wise to keep your

---

[38] Napoleon Hill, *Think and Grow Rich: Original 1937 Edition* (Duke Classics, 2012).

goals to yourself.[39] Deepak Chopra echoes this advice in his 1996 book *The Seven Spiritual Laws of Success*.[40] He, too, suggests keeping your plans to yourself, stating that 'When you seek approval from others, you use energy in a wasteful way'. In other words, we should all be true to ourselves and not seek others' opinions or approval to validate who we are or what we want from life.

Some friends and family members are all too willing to offer 'helpful advice' or 'personal opinions,' and this can derail you, causing you to question your potential or even why you want to achieve these goals in the first place, especially if those people are not aligned with your desires or vision.

This type of advice can knock your confidence or, worse still, cause you to give up. Hill stated that too many people refuse to set high enough goals for themselves for fear of criticism from others, and this is as true today as it was then.[41] People are reluctant to take chances for fear of being laughed at if they don't achieve their desired goal.

For your goals to take on a life of their own, I recommend you apply a strategy to your goal setting. I like the 5Ws and 1H tool. Investigators and journalists commonly use this framework to gather all the necessary information to solve a case or prepare a report. In other words, to tell a story. So, while this is not a typical goal-setting tool, it is a powerful method to help you identify and crystalise your goal by encouraging you to question yourself more deeply: why this goal? Why not something else? Who will benefit when I have achieved my goal? How will I achieve my goal? It will help you design a story or vision that you can convincingly relate

---

[39]   Napoleon Hill, *Think and Grow Rich: Original 1937 Edition* (Duke Classics, 2012).

[40]   Deepak Chopra, *The Seven Spiritual Laws of Success* (Novato, CA: New World Library, 1994).

[41]   Napoleon Hill, *Think and Grow Rich: Original 1937 Edition* (Duke Classics, 2012).

to, and it will help you succinctly tell your 'new life story' and set the scene for your new reality.

Your mind doesn't care what strategy you use when creating your story or even if your story is the truth, so tell it the story of your life and how you want it to be as if you're already living it, believe it, and affirm it regularly.

WOURNAL #13

THE WHEEL OF LIFE EXERCISE

'When your cup is full, stop pouring.'
—Dow

Once you are clear about where your focus should be, take a look at the following wournals about goal setting and see what you think about all the models presented to you. You can decide which model best suits you and which you want to use in your goal-setting practice. To be clear, you don't need to use all the goal-setting models. Select one that you prefer and use that. Most importantly, you must identify your goals and burning desires before you do anything else in the book. You can achieve this by doing the Wheel of Life exercise below.

Wheel of Life courtesy of Madden 2024

---

42   Nina Madden founder of the Courage Coaching Academy, a recognised model first designed by Paul J Meyer in the 1960s.

The above diagram is only an example. You can change the different topics/titles to anything that fits your needs. For example, you may want to avoid working on a goal related to your friendships, so change that to something related to your situation. To use the wheel, score yourself, 1 - not satisfied, 10 - satisfied, by identifying how you feel about each area of your life. The area (s) that score the lowest is the area (s) you should focus on first. Now, you can formulate a goal for this specific area.

CHAPTER 14

TOOL #1: GOAL-SETTING MODELS

'It takes courage to grow up and become who you really are.'
—E.E. Cummings

When you first start setting goals, I would suggest setting your goals for specific sections of the year for those readers who are familiar with the financial year (April - March of the following year), for those of you who are not familiar with the financial year, the year is divided into quarters, each consisting of ninety days. If you're a novice to goal setting, you could think about what you want to achieve within the next ninety days. Sometimes, anything longer than this can seem impossible, too far away, or unachievable, so try to simplify it for yourself initially.

Ninety-day goals provide a realistic timeframe to maintain your focus, considering how busy our lives are nowadays, aiding your success. Achievements positively impact your confidence and self-esteem and, in turn, increase your energy and vibration. If your goal is huge, consider breaking it down into smaller parts, known as chunking down. For example, you might want to set a goal that involves saving £1000 within twelve months. By chunking this down, you could change your goal to saving £250 each quarter; that way, you will achieve something every ninety days, boosting you for more. In the beginning, setting a goal that is too incomprehensible *may* have a negative impact on your mind, and you *might* struggle to accept the possibility of success and, therefore, inadvertently sabotage your efforts.

On the contrary, if you want to set a goal for a year or more, by all means, do so; there are no hard and fast rules here. Sonia Ricotti encourages us to live a maverick life and to set our goals accordingly.[43] She states that we should *stop* being realistic about goal setting and ask ourselves what we want, *not* what we *think* we can achieve. She suggests considering how much money you want to make within twelve months. Remember, it is *not* about how much you *think* you can or *deserve* to make.

Ricotti says that you might not know how you will make the money, but that's not something you should be concerned about right now.[44] Furthermore, she explains that if your goal is to achieve an extra annual income, you must first consider how much you *want* to make and multiply that by ten. For example, you might want to make an extra £50,000 a year; Ricotti suggests multiplying that figure by ten, which would equal £500,000 in this example.

Ricotti's rationale is that if you limit yourself to £50,000, you will dream up ideas worth £50,000. However, if you were working towards £500,000, you would think about ideas to fit that bill instead, and *these* ideas would be far more adventurous, challenging, and exciting.

---

[43]   Sonia Ricotti, 'Eliminate Limiting Beliefs', Webinar attended in January 2024, soniaricotti.com/lifeschool.

[44]   Sonia Ricotti, *Unsinkable: How to Bounce Back Quickly When Life Knocks You Down* (Pompton Plains, NJ: New Page Books, a division of The Career Press, 2015).

THE 5WS AND 1H FRAMEWORK

*'Whatever we plant in our subconscious minds and nourish
with repetition and emotion will one day become our reality.'*
—Earl Nightingale

The premise behind the 5Ws and 1H framework is that once you have answered all six questions, you should have a complete vision of what you want to achieve, why you want to achieve it, and what your new life will look like.

Try to answer the following questions. I have provided some prompts to help, but you may have more that you want to add to each section.

- **What** is your goal? Have a clear vision in mind. What will it cost you if you don't achieve your goal?
- **Why** do you want to achieve this goal? Keep asking yourself *why.* After every answer that you think of, drill deeper into the benefits of why achieving this goal is so important. Repeatedly ask, What is the higher intention of achieving this goal?
- **When** will you achieve this goal? Consider your timeframe for success, go at your own pace, and control your pace. Remember, Rome wasn't built in a day. There is no point in overwhelming yourself. Burnout is indeed real!
- **Who** will benefit when you have achieved your goal? Besides you, who else will benefit? Think broadly. Think about the benefit of the benefit.
- **Where** should you focus your attention? Is there something you need to get out of the way before you can start? Limiting beliefs? Fear? Disempowerment? Negative emotions? On a practical level, do you need to consider childcare arrangements so you can have some

free time? Consider any feelings or thoughts that could stop you from committing to your desire.

- **How** are you going to achieve this goal? Understand the skills and mindset you require to achieve the goal. If needed, look to upskill yourself. If you don't know how to achieve your goal, look for someone to help you. How will you feel when you have achieved your goal?

Be clear about what you want to achieve; clarity is critical here. Writing down that you wish to 'be wealthy' is not enough. Thoroughly consider the 5Ws and 1H framework above.

SMART GOALS

'You're braver than you believe, stronger than you seem, and smarter than you think.'
—A. A. Milne

Another popular goal-setting model is the SMART approach.[45] One I am very familiar with from my clinical days as a physiotherapist.

SMART is an acronym:

- **Specific:** Be clear about what you want to achieve. The more detail you can add here, the better. The Universe loves detail.
- **Measurable:** Add a measure to your goal so that you can see what progress you have made.

---

[45] George T Doran, There's a S.M.A.R.T. way to write managements's goals ..., accessed August 1, 2024, https://community.mis.temple.edu/mis0855002fall2015/files/2015/10/S.M.A.R.T-Way-Management-Review.pdf.

- **Actionable or Achievable:** What actions can you take to achieve your goal? Perhaps some barriers or blocks need to be overcome before you can give your all.
- **Realistic or Relevant:** Your goal should be ambitious, challenging, and stretching, and it should also be relevant to you and the new reality you want to create.
- **Timed:** Set a time frame so you have a target date to work towards. This will give you positive feedback on your success.

Doran's original SMART acronym included Realistic; however, many others have modified the 'R' to mean 'Relevant' over the years. I would suggest that you make your goals realistic and not too outlandish. No matter how hard you try to manifest it, you will never be the Queen of England unless you are Cathryn, HRH Princess of Wales, and you are reading this book!

Finding the best time to set your goals is a personal preference. As we discussed earlier, you can set them for each financial quarter, or you could set them around your birthday or New Year; the choice is yours. The critical thing to mention is once you have set your goals and written them down, you must ensure you consistently revisit them, add to them, make them grow, bring them to life and crucially take action towards achieving them. Even if it's just a few minutes a day, taking action will move you closer to your success and your success closer to you.

A tip from Bob Proctor is to write your goals on a card and keep it in your pocket or purse.[46] Whenever you reach into your pocket or purse, your goal will flash across your mind; read it over and over daily. Repetition will impact your brain cells, and the visuals in your mind will reinforce what you want to achieve.

---

[46] 'Having Goals & Goal Cards—Bob Proctor,' Proctor Gallagher, March 12, 2019, https://www.proctorgallagherinstitute.com/video/having-goals-goal-cards-bob-proctor.

THE GROW MODEL

*'Don't sit down and wait for opportunities
to come. Get up and make them.'*
—Madam CJ Walker

A third popular model is GROW. GROW is another acronym for Goal, Reality, Options and Will. It is a framework used by coaches worldwide for personal development, and it is based on the work that Tim Gallwey, a tennis coach in the United States of America and founder of the Inner Game of Work, completed to assist his professional tennis players.[47]

Gallwey's Inner Game of Work recognised that we have a Self 1 and a Self 2. Self 1 is the supercritical self that gives a running commentary on everything Self 2 does, reminding Self 2 of all its previous failures. It also creates fear and tension when confronted with a challenge. Self 1 creates the worst of the challenges that we face but brazenly puts the blame onto Self 2 and distracts it with negative internal dialogue such as, 'That was rubbish' or 'You'll never be any good at this.'[48]

Gallwey incorporated a workaround for Self 1's continual interference with specific instructions for the tennis player, and what he found was that distracting the player with inconsequential directions quieted the voice of the supercritical Self 1, and, therefore, the player's performance improved. He explains his research as follows: 'The Inner Game is that which takes place in our mind, and is played against such elusive opponents as nervousness, self-doubt and lapses of concentration. It is a game played by your mind against its bad habits. Replacing one pattern

---

[47]   Tim Gallwey, 'The inner game', accessed July 31, 2024, https://www.coachingcultureatwork.com/wp-content/uploads/Tim-Gallweys-The-Inner-Game-1.pdf.

[48]   'Tim Gallwey: The Inner Game,' Culture at Work, August 15, 2023, https://www.coachingcultureatwork.com/tim-gallwey-inner-game-2/.

of mental behaviour with a new, more positive one is the purpose of the Inner Game.' It's worth considering this when we look at self-limiting beliefs later in this book.

In 1979, Sir John Whitmore and Graham Alexander brought the Inner game to Europe, realising that this was a transformational approach for the business world, for managers and leaders of organisations. The pair spent most of the 1980s honing and refining the inner game technique to enhance performance within organisations.[49] The result was a model that assisted people to grow in performance and enjoy learning. So, the GROW model was born. Although this model is used in coaching conversations traditionally, it is something you can work on independently without a coach by working through the four key steps of GROW. It is a straightforward model that will help you identify your goal and any blocks you may have that are sabotaging your efforts and results.

In recent times, the GROW model has been extended to incorporate a T, more commonly known now as the TGROW model. The T is for 'Topic'. Coaches must understand what is going on for the client and establish early on in the session what the client wants to discuss. Therefore, a coaching session would generally start with an open question, such as 'So, what is going on for you?' For the purpose of independent work, I haven't incorporated Topic into the wournal; what I have done is introduce you to the Wheel of Life. This is an excellent way of identifying where your focus should be, particularly if you are feeling overwhelmed or unclear about which goal to start with.

---

[49]   'The Grow Model,' Culture at Work, October 23, 2023, https://www. coachingcultureatwork.com/the-grow-model/.

WOURNAL #14A

SETTING THE 5WS AND 1H GOALS

*'The only way to discover the limits of the possible
is to go beyond them into the impossible.'*
—Arthur C. Clarke

Expected Achievement Date of Goal: _______________________

- **What** is your goal? Think big, empowering, exciting, unlimited and panoramic!

  ____

  ____

  ____

- **Why** do you want to achieve this goal? Why are you motivated to achieve this goal?

  ____

  ____

  ____

- **When** do you want to achieve this goal? Go at your own pace. What is your time frame?

  ____

  ____

  ____

- **Where** should your focus be to achieve your goal? Do you have the correct mindset? Do you have the proper skill set?

  ____

  ____

  ____

  ____

- **Who** will benefit when you have achieved your goal? What is the benefit of the benefit, family, friends, and colleagues?

  ____

  ____

  ____

- **How** much time can you reasonably dedicate to achieving the goal? How will you do this? How are you going to remove any self-limiting blocks you may have? Are there any practical barriers/blocks to overcome? How can you close the gap between where you are now and where you want to be?

  ____

  ____

  ____

  ____

WOURNAL #14B

SETTING SMART GOALS

'To the mind that is still, the whole Universe surrenders.'
—Lao Tzu

- **Specific:** Be clear about what you want to achieve. The more detail you can add here, the better. The Universe loves detail.

____

____

____

____

- **Measurable:** Add a measure to your goal so that you can see clearly what progress you have made.

____

____

____

____

- **Actionable or Achievable:** What actions can you take to achieve your goal? Perhaps some barriers or blocks need to be overcome before you can apply yourself 100 per cent.

____

____

____

____

- **Realistic or Relevant:** Your goal should be ambitious, challenging, and stretching. It should also be relevant to you and the new reality you want to create.

____

____

____

____

- **Timed:** Set a time frame so that you have a target date to work towards. This will give you positive feedback on your success.

____

____

____

____

WOURNAL #14C

USING THE GROW MODEL

'Change your thoughts, and you change the world.'
—Norman Vincent Peale

- **Goal:** What do you want to achieve? What is your goal?

  ____

  ____

  ____

  ____

- **Reality:** Where are you now? How far away are you from achieving your goal? What can you do to close that gap? What have you done previously to achieve this goal? What resources do you have or need to accomplish this goal?

  ____

  ____

  ____

  ____

- **Options:** What could you do to achieve your goal? Explore all the different options that come to mind.

  ____

  ____

  ____

- **Will:** What will you do? What is your way forward? On a scale of 1 to 10, how committed are you to taking this plan forward?

  ____

  ____

  ____

  ____

This chapter has introduced several goal-setting models. You don't need to use all of them; select which one resonates with you the most and use that approach. You're doing great work. Let's keep the momentum going and look at self-limiting beliefs. This section will help you identify where those barriers and blocks are so that you can raise your awareness of them and overcome them for your greater good.

CHAPTER 15

TOOL #2:
SELF-LIMITING BELIEFS

'A dead end is just a good place to turn around.'
—Naomi Judd

In this section, you will learn about self-limiting beliefs, how they are developed, and, more importantly, how to overcome them by controlling our minds and thoughts. Let's jump straight in; self-limiting beliefs are those beliefs that hold us back from our true potential. They are the self-deprecating negative thoughts, the internal dialogue we have running through our minds all day and every day. For example, 'I don't deserve happiness', 'I am too stupid to build my own business', or 'I am rubbish with money'.

How many of us have grown up with our parents/guardians/ society saying, 'Money doesn't grow on trees', 'I'm not made of money' or 'Money is the root of all evil'? This constant message is one of lack and scarcity. How many of us were told, 'You'll never amount to anything', or perhaps one of your parents left home when you were very young, and you have questioned why your whole life, 'Was I not worth staying around for?'

Did the adults around you encourage you to be the best you can be? Or was there a subliminal message such as, 'Things like that don't happen to people like us' or 'You weren't born with a silver spoon in your mouth' or perhaps 'We are not privileged like them'? This may come as a shock, but we are all programmed by these attitudes and misaligned messages, which only keep you from achieving what is rightfully yours, your true potential, what you were put on the earth to achieve! I am not saying that any of this subliminal messaging was malicious. Unfortunately, our elders didn't know better back then, but *we* do now. So, if you want a new life or to make changes, you must change your programming. Furthermore, to those readers with young children, nieces and nephews, or grandchildren, a polite word of caution: be mindful of the messages you are sending to the young people in your life to avoid history repeating itself.

For those of you thinking, 'That's it, I am doomed because of my self-limiting beliefs, ' there's good news! Assaraf states that your brain is not fixed; it can adapt and change if we encourage it to do so.[50] However, this reprogramming of your brain takes time, anywhere from sixty-six days to three hundred and sixty-five days. It won't happen overnight, so please be patient with yourself!

The brain's ability to adapt over time is known as neuroplasticity, something I became familiar with when working in stroke rehabilitation as a physiotherapist. Just as stroke survivors' brains can adapt and relearn fundamental tasks such as walking, talking, and eating, our non-injured brains can also adjust. It can learn to override our limiting beliefs, reset our self-image, and improve our skills. But first, we must change our mindset *and* skill set and take action. Otherwise, we will be pulled back into our old ways and back into our comfort zones, where our brains feel safe and secure.[51]

---

[50]   John Assaraf, *Innercise: The New Science to Unlock Your Brain's Hidden Power* (Cardiff, CA: Waterside Press, 2018).

[51]   John Assaraf, *Innercise: The New Science to Unlock Your Brain's Hidden Power* (Cardiff, CA: Waterside Press, 2018).

POSITIVITY ON THE MIND

'You are not a body; you have a body.'
—Dolores Cannon

Proctor talks about the complexities of the mind. He said, 'There is a power that comes into our conscious mind, causing us to think anything we want to think, resulting in thoughts being generated, which subsequently impact our subconscious minds, and in turn create feelings that impact the physical body causing us to act, ultimately generating a result.'[52] That's a little tricky to understand, so perhaps read that again.

Proctor suggested that underpinning all of this is our attitude. We can see the negative or the positive in anything we view, but we will only see the positives with the right attitude. The way we see things is based on our internal belief system, and this is a direct result of our own experiences. The conscious mind is the thinking, educated mind, also known as the intellectual mind. It can accept or reject anything it is presented with. The subconscious mind, on the other hand, is our emotional mind. It is not as refined as the conscious mind, and so it must accept everything it is presented with; it *cannot* reject anything. What you impress on the subconscious mind gets you the results you desire. It cannot differentiate between what is real, unreal, or imagined. Most people don't understand how to manipulate this. Therefore, they continue to think about what is wrong or what they don't want.

Negative information flows into the conscious mind, but because most people don't truly think and reject what is inflicted upon them, it leaves the subconscious mind wide open to absorb all the negative information it is receiving from society, from places

---

[52] 'Law of Vibration (Full Lesson): Bob Proctor', YouTube, April 12, 2021, https://youtu.be/-ENj3vyFvKo.

like the news, social media, television, films and music. Since the subconscious mind cannot reject anything, this information is easily absorbed, believed, and held within the brain forever unless we *choose* to no longer believe these things. It is our choice to hold onto these beliefs, or we can choose to heal ourselves and remove them from our belief systems once and for all. So why do so many of us keep hold of them? Indeed, this is self-sabotage. Ultimately, a belief is only a thought that we continually repeat in our minds.

Unfortunately, we are programmed to live this way. This is our paradigm, a mental programme that has almost exclusive control over our habitual behaviour, and nearly all of our behaviour is habitual. As infants, we were exposed to many things: love, hate, different languages, and the limiting messages we received. Since our conscious minds weren't mature enough to reject anything, this information was poured into our subconscious minds, which were wide open.

Proctor continues, 'We have all gathered an abundance of knowledge through our educational system, covering numerous subjects, but little has anything to do with this paradigm. Therefore, we frequently do not do what we already know how to do. Superior knowledge drives inferior results, in turn, causing confusion and frustration.' This is why some people with qualifications, as long as their arms are poor, while others with very little education, are rich. Why, I hear you ask? Well, that's a very good question! It's all due to the programming we received before we could think for ourselves.

CHANGE THE PARADIGM

'You need nothing to be happy. You need something to be sad.'
—Mooji

So, if you want to change your results, you must change the paradigm of your habitual behaviour. Proctor advises us not to allow our paradigms to control us. We can create the life we want, but first, we must decide what life that is and then say no to everything else that isn't it.

There is a spiritual perfection inside each of us, but our paradigms suppress this, so it struggles to express itself. Our spiritual perfection is always seeking expression within us and through us, and this is why we always want more for our lives. Proctor suggested that we should not focus on wanting to 'get'. Human growth is what most of us want, and by bringing more of our spiritual perfection to the table, the 'getting' is a positive consequence of the want. The want gives birth to the desire. The more you feed the desire, the stronger it becomes.

Desire is the unexpressed possibility within us, seeking its expression through the body and into action, which gets results. Personal growth and development are the fundamental desires of human beings. We all have a burning desire to improve our lives and ourselves. Furthermore, many of us seek the answer to the ultimate question: 'What is my life's purpose?' With this in mind, we should set out to personally develop and grow; consequently, we encourage others to grow and develop alongside us.

Now that we have discussed the impact our paradigms have on our lives and on our behaviours, we understand that to have a happier, more successful life, we must let go of the negative beliefs we all carry. By telling our subconscious minds a different story, we are forcing our brains to adapt and change, which will positively impact our realities.

Phew, that was deep! Let's jump into the wournal and explore your personal self-limiting beliefs. When you're finished with that, I will also introduce another coaching model that you can use for self-exploration, the Looping Thought Ladder.[53]

[53]   'Rapid Transformational Therapy: RTT Courses & Training Cost', Marisa Peer, January 9, 2024, https://marisapeer.com/rtt-training-courses/.

WOURNAL #15A

SELF-LIMITING BELIEFS EXERCISE

'Your beliefs are yours to change.'
—Marisa Peer

Self-limiting beliefs are those little pearls of wisdom 'lovingly' offered by other people, those beliefs that have been *given* to you, and you have *chosen* to believe because you didn't know any better, but now they no longer serve you.[54]

It's time to upgrade those beliefs right now.

- **What lies do you tell yourself?**

  ____

  ____

  ____

  ____

- **What are your limiting beliefs? Where do they come from?**

  ____

  ____

  ____

  ____

- **How can you change these beliefs into something more positive that serves you better now?**

  ____

  ____

  ____

---

[54] 'I Will Teach You How to Destroy Your Negative Thoughts & Feelings Today': Marisa Peer,' YouTube, January 25, 2021, https://youtu.be/4ku0R6ZW0NM?si=R0pDxEDPkp9buNdy.

WOURNAL #15B

LOOPING THOUGHT LADDER

'He who says he can and he who says
he can't are both usually right.'
—Confucius

This is the Looping Thought Ladder.[55] It demonstrates how your thoughts impact your feelings, which affects your actions and, in turn, affects your thoughts. For a moment, consider that your negative thought is something like, 'Success is not available to me.' These six words are what is holding you back from changing your reality. This thought is misaligned with your goal, and as the ladder demonstrates, it will impact your feelings and actions. Your mind will seek out evidence to support your negative statement.

Consider what or how you can change this negative Looping Thought Ladder into a more positive one. Try changing one of those words. In fact, it's not even a word; it is a letter that is incorporated into something positive and aligned with your goal. (Hint! Change *not* to *now*.)

Reframe your statement into 'Success is now available to me.' Think about what feeling that conjures up. One of excitement? Motivation? Then consider these new feelings: What actions will you take, inspired? Creative? Happy to try new things? A newfound confidence, perhaps? Now, what is your mind saying to you? 'Success is now available to me.' From now on, keep *that* thought looping around your mind and see how much better you feel. If you would like a more detailed

---

[55] 'RTT Rapid Transformational Therapy: Marisa Peer Method Hypnotherapy,' Rapid Transformational Therapy: RTT®, January 9, 2024, https://rtt.com/.

way of changing your thought patterns, the CBT exercise in the book may just help.

CHAPTER 16

TOOL #3:
GRACIOUS GRATITUDE

'Out of a mountain of despair, a stone of hope.'
—Martin Luther King

The importance of being grateful for all we have cannot be underestimated. Over many decades, research studies have been published, all of which have supported the hypothesis that gratitude positively impacts human beings' wellness. Although research into this area of gratitude is still relatively new, there are many benefits of practising gratitude, such as improving relationships, physical and psychological health, empathy and a reduction in aggression. People who practise gratitude report sleeping better than those who don't. It enhances self-esteem and mental resilience.[56] So, counting your blessings and consistently practising gratitude profoundly affects the mind and behaviour.

---

[56] '7 Scientifically Proven Benefits of Gratitude', Psychology Today, accessed July 31, 2024, https://www.psychologytoday.com/us/blog/what-mentally-strong-people-dont-do/201504/7-scientifically-proven-benefits-of-gratitude.

What you decide to show gratitude for is entirely up to you, but here are a few ideas to get you started:

- Your partner (husband, wife, boyfriend, or girlfriend).
- Your job (the work you do, the money you earn, your colleagues, your boss).
- The place you live (where you are dry, warm and safe).
- Friends and all the memories you have shared with them (happy or sad).
- Parents/guardians/caregivers and the love they have shown you.
- Physical attributes (eyes, ears, arms and legs).
- Material things (car, handbags, shoes).
- Animals (pets, birds in your garden, squirrels in the park).

We can be grateful for almost anything and everything; there is no limit. The key to this is to look around you, see what you already have in your life, and appreciate every little thing.

I have a small wooden plaque on my desk that my son bought for me that reads, 'Never let the things you want make you forget the things you already have.' I believe the quote comes from Sanchita Pandey, and there's never been a truer word said. How many of us go through life looking for the next best thing, bigger, shinier, and more expensive than the last thing we wanted? It's okay; we are all friends here, and I am just as guilty as the next person. I think my son may have been trying to send me a message with this plaque, and in a not-so-subtle way! So, in the true essence of gratitude … *Thank you.*

GUILTY PLEASURES

'If you don't like the road you're walking,
start paving another one.'
—Dolly Parton

I am a nightmare when it comes to buying shoes. I'm not quite to the extreme as Imelda Marcos, but I'm getting there. I have been known to fall in love with a pair of shoes in the shop. I have gone *crazy* for them and had to have them. I was only ever going to be happy if they were in my possession, and then, I would wear them once and start looking for another pair to buy. Maybe your guilty pleasure isn't shoes, but I bet you have one!

What is that all about? We no sooner get what we so desperately want than the shine falls off it, and we look for the next best thing. So, the lesson for the day is this: Gratitude helps us refocus on what we have and *not* on what we lack. It's a work in progress; it is in my case.

Now that I have aired my dirty laundry, it's time for you to complete the wournal on the next page. Good luck! Don't worry; you don't have to share it with anyone if you don't want to.

WOURNAL #16A

GRACIOUS GRATITUDE EXERCISE

'Positive anything is better than negative nothing.'
—Elbert Hubbard

Think about all the good things you already have in your life, and wournal your gratitude. An old-fashioned saying that we should all incorporate into our lives more often is to 'count your blessings'. What blessings do you want to count? What are you grateful for right now? Why are you grateful for these things? How do you feel about these things, the people, the relationships you have in your life?

Each day, write one sentence about what it is you are grateful for, and repeat this sentence numerous times throughout the day, with feelings and emotions attached.

WOURNAL #16B

A LETTER TO THE UNIVERSE

'Try to be a rainbow in someone else's cloud.'
—Maya Angelou

This exercise combines your goals with gratitude. Consider writing a letter to the Universe, Source, or God, whichever name you prefer to use, where you express thanks for all you have now in your life. Express gratitude for the help you have received for the life you are living now, and incorporate the vision you have for your future. Write your appreciation of the future vision as though you already have it and are living it.

Dear Universe/Source/God,

____

____

____

____

____

____

____

____

____

____

____

____

____

Signed with Blessings and Light

CHAPTER 17

TOOL #4:
VISUALISATION

'If you do what you have always done,
you get what you have always got.'
—Mark Twain

In my quest to learn more about visualisation, I discovered a YouTube video by Quazi Johir, founder of Realitycreator. com.[57] Johir describes the journey he has been on, from being broke to earning $20,000 a month, using a method of visualisation, and he walks you through it step by step.

This amazing video explains the visualisation process in much more detail than I have ever heard. He explains how to visualise properly and more effectively to achieve better results. My experience of visualisation, to date, has involved finding somewhere quiet and taking a few deep breaths in and out while focusing on my goal and what I wanted to achieve. Johir's video takes you *way* beyond that technique.

A lot of subject matter experts, such as Abraham Hicks and Bob Proctor, advise us to participate in visualisation

---

[57] 'Once I Learned How to Visualise Correctly, I Became a Millionaire (the Truth)', YouTube, January 23, 2024, https://youtu.be/IO0RfHBu3IE.

regularly.[58], [59]When done in a certain way, it can move you towards achieving your goal. It helps us feel attuned to our goals and the reality we wish to create for ourselves. If you can align your heart and mind to feel the associated feelings that things are improving, leading you towards goal achievement, everything that you have, everything that you do, and every move you make will be directed toward achieving your goal and living the life your inner self desires.

The process Johir recommends is composed of three parts, which are pretty detailed, so stay with me.

---

[58] Manifestation Motivations, "17 Seconds Is All It Takes To Manifest The Thing You Want - Abraham Hicks," YouTube, December 6, 2022, https://youtu.be/DQq3vOmbwTc?si=XnkeNXt9WK1NZUF7.

[59] 'Tell Us What You Want, We'll Show You How to Get It,' Proctor Gallagher, July 18, 2024, http://www.proctorgallagherinstitute.com/.

WOURNAL #17

VISUALISATION EXERCISE

'If my mind can conceive it, if my heart can believe it, then I can achieve it.'
—Muhammad Ali

Consider this: you decide you want to buy a particular item. In my case, this might be shoes. You look for it online, and you place your order. You then wait for the order to be dispatched and delivered to you. What you don't do is sit there stressing and worrying, wondering if your parcel will arrive. You trust in the process, and you are patient. Apply the same strategy to your burning desires, and be patient. They will get delivered. Put simply, decide what you are going to have as if it is already done. It is guaranteed. Assume it is going to happen.

Step 1: Visualise your reality.

- Prioritise one of your goals or your only goal. Perhaps you have a goal that would fulfil many other goals, such as, like Johir, you, too, want to earn 20,000 a month. This would mean that you could give up the job you hate so much, set yourself up in your business, buy that bigger house, or send your children to a private school. Whatever your goal is, visualise what *that* would look like when you have achieved it. Visualise getting into that Porsche each morning to drive your children to that fancy private school, feel the emotions attached to *that,* and do this exercise every morning and every night.
- Consider one step that you know you can take right now that could take you forward to achieving your goal. It could be that you need to learn a new skill or do more

research. Now, visualise yourself doing *that*. Visualise signing up for an online course, logging on to study, and successfully achieving the course with a *distinction*. Remember to aim high!

- The intention is a *firm* resoluteness in your decision to have or achieve something, and it is broken down into two components:
  1. Inner Intention: Your personal resolve to 'Focus on doing something to get something'.
  2. Outer Intention: Your personal resolve to have something, no matter how it happens, the 'Focus on how the outcome gets achieved, of its own accord'.

Tip: Use **inner intention** to execute the process and **outer intention** to focus on the milestones achieved.

Step 2: Visualise your ideal self.

- Self-inquiry: What does your new ideal self look like?
- Define your new self.
- What five superpowers would this new you have?
  - Identify *five* key traits that they would have that perhaps the 'old' you *does not* possess or possibly *does* possess but not in high enough quantities.
  - What habits would this new you have? What would their day-to-day schedule look like?
  - What style of character would this person have? Would they buy cheap clothes or more expensive clothes? How would they conduct themselves?

Step 3: Embodiment: Ask yourself how this ideal self/new you would do specific things, such as:

- Conducting a task.
- Making decisions.

Tip: We've all heard the saying 'fake it until you make it'. Well, now is that time. Knock yourself out and have fun. Pretend to be this new you/ideal self, and remember who you pretend to be *is* who you will become.

'The more clear and definite you make your picture, and the more you dwell upon it, bringing out all its delightful details, the stronger your desire will be; and the stronger your desire, the easier it will be to hold your mind fixed upon the picture of what you want.'[60]

Now, I am not for one minute suggesting that you should go out and buy a new expensive outfit to 'look the part', but you could consider tucking in your T-shirt, wiping over those trainers with a damp cloth, or simply ensuring your hands and nails are clean. Small, simple things to shift your mind towards the most successful person you want to become *can* make all the difference in how you feel and how you act, and it doesn't have to cost any money.

---

[60]　Wallace D. Wattles and Fauun, *The Science of Getting Rich* (La Vergne: Fauun, 2024).

CHAPTER 18

TOOL #5:
POSITIVE AFFIRMATIONS

'It's never too late to be what you might have been.'
—George Eliot

Affirmations have long been promoted as a form of self-help. Through repetition of positive self-talk, we can reprogramme our subconscious minds into believing something better. Earlier in the book, we talked about the subconscious mind being unable to reject anything that it is told. Well, this is where positive affirmations come into play. Through daily affirmations, we can convince our minds of a better reality. Positive affirmations help us to overcome fear and reduce self-sabotage. Furthermore, they allow us to rewrite the negative, repetitive chatter that runs through our minds.

As Assaraf suggests, it can take between sixty-six days to three hundred and sixty-five days for the brain to be rewired.[61] Therefore, you should commit to practising positive affirmations for that duration to allow your brain to accept this as the new norm. Have faith in the process and keep an open mind to it.

---

[61] John Assaraf, *Innercise: The New Science to Unlock Your Brain's Hidden Power* (Cardiff, CA: Waterside Press, 2018).

Don't let your rational conscious mind jump in and override you with statements like 'This will never work' or 'Who are you trying to kid?'

Remember Tim Gallwey's Inner Game: Self 1, which is super critical of Self 2? Dolores Cannon referred to this negative, doubtful voice coming from the left side of the brain as 'Mr. Stupid', and suggested that he always wants to jump in and give you his two penneth![62] Push it to one side, ignore it, and carry on regardless.

Assaraf refers to this concept as your Frankenstein brain and your Einstein brain, or the Stein brothers! Frankenstein is our negative brain and is highly reactive, the part that instils fear into us with comments like 'What if I fail, make a fool of myself, get criticised, or get laughed at?'. At the same time, our Einstein brain is far more positive and excitable, a real *go-getter.* 'Yay, we can do this. This is going to work. Let me do it!'

Remember that *you* are a master manifester and a co-creator of *your* reality alongside the Universe, and nothing, I repeat, *nothing* is impossible. By dedicating yourself to this process, you are setting out your intentions clearly and inviting the Universe to provide you with inspiration, opportunities, and resources to fulfil your desires.

NIKOLA TESLA

Nikola Tesla was a Serbian-American inventor and engineer born in 1856. He is most famous for discovering the rotating magnetic field, which is the basis of the alternating current (AC) within machinery. He was responsible for the three-phase electric power transmission system and later invented the Tesla coil, an induction

---

[62] 'QHHT {Quantum Healing Hypnosis Technique} Official Training,' QHHT Official Website, July 1, 2024, http://QHHTofficial.com/.

coil used in radio transmission.[63] All of Tesla's inventions radically affected life, and they still do in our modern day.

Despite his groundbreaking inventions, Tesla had a fascination with the significance of numbers, in particular the numbers 3, 6, and 9, but this area of his work was often overlooked.[64] Tesla theorised that these three numbers could unlock the secrets of the Universe. He suggested that the numbers 3, 6, and 9 were the Universe's building blocks and that they had a profound effect on all things, from energy to frequency and the structure of matter. Tesla suggested that only these numbers could exist as energy without losing their identity. Modern-day physics now supports this concept, so Tesla set about using these numbers to crack the secrets of the Universe and devised the 3-6-9 theory for manifestation through a three-step approach towards the practice of positive affirmations.

Pinon stated that the synchronicity of these numbers is *directly* correlated with the Universe.[65] Pinon explains that the number three is directly linked to the Universe/source or God, the number six represents the most profound strength we have within us, and the number nine is related to letting go of the past and moving on. Furthermore, it helps us to release any negativity or feelings of self-doubt.

Let's dive into a famous method relating to positive affirmations: the 3-6-9 method designed by Nikola Tesla.

---

[63] 'Nikola Tesla', Encyclopædia Britannica, June 16, 2024, https://www.britannica.com/biography/Nikola-Tesla.

[64] Medium, accessed July 31, 2024, https://brandtamela.medium.com/unlocking-the-secrets-of-369-understanding-teslas-theory-of-numbers.

[65] Susie Pinon, 'Manifest Anything with the 3–6–9 Manifestation Method', Medium, February 16, 2022, https://medium.com/the-orange-journal/manifest-anything-with-the-3-6-9-manifestation-method-1aee29bf24c7.

TESLA'S 3-6-9 METHOD

*'If you want to find the secrets of the Universe, think
in terms of energy, frequency, and vibration.'*
—Nikola Tesla

Step 1: Choose a strong and positive affirmation supporting your goals and write it down three times. Your affirmations should be clear, concise, and specific.

For example:

- I am so happy and grateful now that abundance flows to me.
- I am thrilled and grateful now that I am running my own successful business.
- I am open and ready to have a loving and respectful relationship.

Each morning, write these affirmations down three times.

Step 2: Each lunchtime, repeat your positive affirmation statement six times, say it out loud, and/or write it down six times, allowing seventeen seconds for each one to penetrate the subconscious mind.

- Seventeen seconds of pure thought is all it takes to kick-start the manifestation process.[66] If you have a goal for a loving relationship, as you repeat your positive affirmation, let your heart fill up with the feeling and gratitude of having that special person in your life right now.
- As we have learnt, your subconscious mind cannot differentiate between what is real and what is not, so if you believe that something is, you can begin to rewire

---

[66] '17 Seconds Is All It Takes to Manifest the Thing You Want - Abraham Hicks', YouTube, December 6, 2022, https://youtu.be/DQq3vOmbwTc?si=yz7HAlNWb2_CHZ6C.

your brain and your subconscious mind towards that desire and who you want to become. As infinite divine beings, we must transcend our perceived limitations and realise our true full potential to manifest peace, love, and harmony into our lives and the Universe.

- Align yourself with the vibration of already having what you desire, and speak them into existence through repetition of your positive affirmations.
- I find it useful to set my phone or add a meeting time to my Outlook calendar, blocking off the time to focus on my affirmations. Especially if, like me, you work from home and often miss lunchtime.

Step 3: Before bed, write your affirmations and recite them out loud nine times. This step is crucial because, while we are sleeping, our brain organises our thoughts and the information that we have accumulated throughout the day. Doing this before sleep allows those words to sit in your brain, percolating and influencing your subconscious mind, undisturbed whilst you are sleeping.

In this section, we have discussed the 3-6-9 method and how to implement it into your daily routine. It's time to wournal your positive affirmations, and in the words of our Einstein brains … *let's go!*

WOURNAL #18

POSITIVE AFFIRMATION EXERCISE

'Choose to be optimistic. It feels better.'
—Dali Lama

Step 1. Morning Routine: What positive affirmations do you want to tell yourself? Write it out three times.

____

____

____

Step 2. Afternoon Routine: Write or say your affirmations out loud six times, allowing seventeen seconds between each one.

____

____

____

Step 3. Before Bed: Write or say out loud your affirmations nine times.

____

____

____

CHAPTER 19

TOOL #6:
COGNITIVE BEHAVIOURAL
THERAPY (CBT)

*'Great things happen to those who don't stop believing,
trying, learning and being grateful.'*
—Roy T. Bennett

A number of years ago, I was bullied by a so-called friend who happened to be a colleague. For anonymity, I will call her 'Susie'. One day, I discovered that Susie had lied to me about an affair she was having with another colleague of ours behind her new husband's back. I hear you ask, 'What business is that of yours?' Well, on the surface, that is very true, and quite frankly, I didn't care who she was sleeping with. But what I did care about was how it had made me look to our other colleagues when the gossip was rife, and I had defended her to the hilt.

When I discovered the truth, I was hurt and embarrassed for being so gullible and believing in my friend, so I told Susie how it had affected me. In retaliation, Susie and her 'boyfriend' thought it would be a good idea to steal my photographs from my Facebook profile and make up a false account on the dating website Plenty of Fish, unbeknown to me. I have no idea how long the account was live, but one Saturday afternoon, I was having lunch with a friend when my mobile phone started pinging with lots of different messages from numbers I did not recognise. Some messages were much less pleasant than others, and all of them were from men.

I had no idea what was going on, and my mind was in turmoil. I decided to respond to one of the more pleasant messages, asking who he was and why he was messaging me. He informed me that 'we' had just been talking on Plenty of Fish! I quickly replied and told him I was not on any dating website and that there must have been some mistake. The man informed me of the profile on this site, and the person behind it was giving out my telephone number. I was horrified. Suddenly, it all made sense, and I baulked at the idea that someone had put me on a dating website without my consent, and consequently, people I didn't know were harassing me.

Now, to cut a long story short, this incident impacted my mental health massively. I know now I shouldn't have let it, but I did. When this happened, I lived alone, and I suspected that since those responsible had given out my phone number, then they could quite easily have provided strangers with my home address, too. I worried about unscrupulous people turning up at my house. I became extremely anxious and paranoid due to the 'trauma', and I was unable to go to work, becoming isolated, which ultimately led to depression. Through my employer, I gained access to a fantastic therapist who introduced me to cognitive behavioural therapy or CBT, as most people know it. By following my therapist's advice and guidance over time, I became well again, returning to work and socialising, and my life now is unrecognisable from what it was back then. So, the long and short of it is that this really worked for me. It is a well-established, highly-researched technique that is widely used by mental health professionals.

It was through writing this book that I started to think that some principles of CBT could help others with negative thought processes, self-sabotage, and imposter syndrome, even if there is no suggestion of depression or anxiety in the individual. I have used this technique many times over the years, and in a variety of ways, not just because of anxiety or depression, but when I have become aware that I am having a negative dialogue internally within my mind. So, if you permit me, I would like to introduce you to CBT and the exercise I completed, which helped me on my wellness journey and toward a much better reality.

CBT focuses on your thoughts, emotions and behaviours. As we have already established, how we think impacts how we feel and our behaviours. Conversely, how we behave impacts how we think, which affects how we feel. Let's look at a simple example: you know you should be going to the gym on your way home from work, but you don't feel up to it, so you don't go. In this example, your thoughts and feelings have affected your behaviour. Now, let's look at this from a different perspective, using the same example: even though you don't really want to go to the gym on the way home from work, you go anyway. Afterwards, you feel energised and happy, your mood is lifted, and you give yourself a little pat on the back for going, so now your behaviour has positively impacted your thoughts and feelings. Simple!

UNHEALTHY BEHAVIOURS

'Let us make our future now, and let us make
our dreams tomorrow's reality.'
—Malala Yousafzai

Heffernan talks about two different types of unhealthy behaviour: compulsive and avoidant.[67] Compulsive behaviour involves working long hours, overeating and/or drinking too much

---

[67]   'Cognitive Behavioral Therapy Exercises (Feel Better!)', YouTube, August 13, 2019, https://youtu.be/3VIL1L_ypMg.

alcohol, whereas avoidant behaviour includes things like not going out of the house to avoid going places and being seen, which results in isolation and potentially depression. Procrastination is another type of avoidant fear-based behaviour that pops up, especially if, like me, you are a perfectionist and you fear that your work won't be perfect. This resonated with me in terms of writing this book. I had a goal to have this book written by the end of 2023; however, it is now May 2024, and I am still writing it! I understand now that this is solely down to my tendencies of perfectionism, as it has to be right before I can let anyone read it. This fear plays out in procrastination, so my behaviour has been one of avoidance.

So, back to my tale, I would say that avoidant behaviours were present then, too, since I isolated myself and didn't go to work or see friends. Heffernan informs us that both behaviours are destructive, and neither works for our highest good. They force us to pretend that things aren't happening, so we numb our feelings and sublimate our issues. This will only serve to reinforce fear and anxiety.

HEALTHY BEHAVIOURS

*'Happiness is not something readymade; it
comes from your own actions.'*
—The Dalai Lama

Let's touch briefly on healthy behaviours and consider what they look like. Heffernan suggests that healthy behaviours are doing things like calling a friend, going for a walk, asking for help with a task, meditation or yoga, or even something as simple as hugging your pet.[68] It is for you to decide what your healthy behaviours

---

[68]   'Cognitive Behavioral Therapy Exercises (Feel Better!)', YouTube, August 13, 2019, https://youtu.be/3VIL1L_ypMg.

look like. Changing your behaviour is vital to feeling better and reducing your negative internal dialogue. Adopting healthy behaviours is critical to rewiring your brain. It communicates with the 'old' brain and reprogrammes your emotional brain. We must remember that our behaviours do not have to be driven by our feelings and thoughts.

It isn't easy to change the way we think. It takes time and practice, but by using a CBT technique, we can identify where we can intervene, either with our thought patterns or our behaviours.[69]

This concept leads us nicely into the CBT exercise. If you have negative thoughts that impact your goal achievement, try the CBT log on the next page. This is the same one I used in my therapy. See if you can reframe these thoughts into more positive ones, which could then become a positive affirmation that you could apply to Tesla's 3-6-9 method.

---

[69] 'Cognitive Behavioral Therapy Exercises (Feel Better!)', YouTube, August 13, 2019, https://youtu.be/3VIL1L_ypMg.

WOURNAL #19

CBT EXERCISE

'You are a mass of energy, and you function on frequencies.'
—Leland Val Van de Wall

Step 1: Situation: Describe the issue. What has or is happening for/to you?

____

____

____

____

Step 2: Identify feelings: emotional and physical.
- **Label** the emotion.
- **Score** that emotion on a scale of 1 to 10 (circle one).

Low 1 2 3 4 5 6 7 8 9 10 High

- **Score** your physical feelings on a scale of 1 10 (circle one)

Low 1 2 3 4 5 6 7 8 9 10 High

- Notice any physical feelings you have and wournal them here. Do you have pain or headaches, perhaps?

____

____

____

____

Step 3: Identify unhelpful thoughts and unhelpful behaviours.
- What are your unhelpful **thoughts?** Write them down.
- Note any unhelpful **behaviour,** compulsive or avoidant.

____

____

____

____

Tip: I was also encouraged to identify any evidence that supported my negative self-talk. Your unconscious mind will always seek proof to support your negativity.

- **Write about any evidence you have found that supports the negative talk in your mind. Is there any?**

____

____

____

____

Step 4: Identify alternative thoughts and behaviours.
- Reframe your thoughts towards the positive and away from the negative.
- What would you say to your friend? We wouldn't speak to our friends in the same way as we speak to ourselves.
- Look for a healthy behaviour alternative. What does this look like for you?

____

____

____

____

Step 5: Identify your feelings after these alternative thoughts and behaviours.
- How do you feel now that there has been a shift in your thinking or behaviour?
- Score your **new** emotion on a scale of 1 to 10 (circle one).

Low 1 2 3 4 5 6 7 8 9 10 High

- Note your **new** physical feeling on a scale of 1 to 10 (circle one).

Low 1 2 3 4 5 6 7 8 9 10 High

- Compare this new score to your original feeling in Step 2.
- **Make notes of any shift or changes you recognise in yourself.**

____

____

____

____

Well done! It's not easy to change your thinking, but **go you!** You're doing it!

During the writing process of this book, I experienced severe imposter syndrome. I would regularly tell myself, 'What do you know about writing a book?' or 'For goodness sake, stick to your day job!' I regularly visited this exercise to search for any evidence that supported the negative self-talk that I had going on in my mind. I looked for evidence to support why I *couldn't* write a book. I would reframe this self-talk into 'Many other people do, so why not me? Established authors started somewhere', or 'Why shouldn't I spread my wings and develop myself?'. I would often revisit the poem at the front of the book by Marianne Williamson just to remind myself of my greatness. My ultimate goal was to provide a service to others, therefore, if you are reading this book right now, boom! My mission has been accomplished, and it shows that my negative internal dialogue was unfounded, and it *tried* its damndest to derail me through procrastination and fear. But it didn't win. *Don't* let it get the better of you.

FINAL THOUGHTS

Well done, and way to go! If you are reading this now, it must mean you have finished the book. I genuinely hope that you have enjoyed working your way through the Universal Laws and the wournal, and I really hope you have learnt things you didn't already know. I wish you every success with implementing the Universal Laws and the exercises you have completed.

Before you leave, though, I wanted to share with you another personal tale; while writing this book, I received some unfortunate news from my employer that I was being made redundant. CRIKEY! What are you going to do? I hear you ask. Well, I picked up this book and I reminded myself of each of the Universal Laws, and I put each one of them into practice, using the wournals as I went. My friends and family were *gobsmacked* with my positive mental attitude and almost blase approach to losing my job.

I reminded myself that the way we feel and act is a choice. I could choose to worry and fret over the loss of my job, or I could try to identify what the experience was teaching me. Panicking, worrying, and stressing would not help my mind to think clearly, and I would not be able to work out my options.

Furthermore, I reflected on the Law of Divine Oneness and reminded myself that despite my hurt and disappointment—not to mention anger—I was divinely connected to the senior executive sitting in front of me while delivering the hammer blow. As I sat there listening to the pre-planned script about the buy and build strategy of the company, I mentally and quietly blessed them in my mind. I considered Caroline Flack's lasting words—#BeKind—I also reminded myself, 'If I hurt you, I hurt myself.' Of course, I don't mean physically … or do I?

I thought about how grateful I was for the opportunity of employment with the company for the past two years, and I quietly expressed gratitude to the Universe for—not so subtly—nudging me towards finishing writing this book through the Law of Inspired Action. Also, I was grateful for the intuition to make a start when I did—which, of course, my goals, visualisation and positive affirmations were all geared towards the book, making me some money and helping others! Well, that is what the Law of Compensation decrees, isn't it? It states that we will be compensated for our efforts … in time. Not to mention the Law of Attraction … right?

I considered how the Law of Attraction and the Law of Correspondence had played a part in creating my reality. Over the last twelve months, the company had been continually restructuring, and as a result, I had experienced an undeniable nagging fear—and plenty of negative thoughts—about how it was only a matter of time until the axe of redundancy was falling in my direction, then out of the blue: BANG! It happened.

So, my fears and anxiety about losing my job had been realised: constantly thinking about what I didn't want delivered exactly what I didn't want! I set about enlisting all the laws, including the Law of Polarity, whereby there are two opposite ends of a scale and two different ways of viewing things—either negatively or positively—I looked for the silver lining in my cloud and I found it. I understood through my lived experience all about the Law of Perpetual Transmutation of Energy because everything is changing—including my employment status—and I transformed my energy into a positive one.

I reiterated the concepts of the Law of Relativity to my friends and family, and I concluded that my glass was indeed half-full. I had a lot to be grateful for, and I could use this temporary setback as an opportunity for growth and not as a detriment to myself. I was determined not to plunge into a pit of despair. As the Law of Rhythm reminds us, life has its challenges—it ebbs and flows—and as a problematic challenge occurs, we must have faith that better times are on the way.

With all this in mind, I maintained a high vibration. I continued to take inspired action when applying for jobs; I focused on completing my book and building my own coaching and NLP business. At the time of writing these final words, I remain employed by the company—but not for much longer—so I can't provide you with an update on how the job hunt is going and how successful I have been in any interviews. Still, I know and trust that the Universe has a plan, that it is in hand, and that I *will* be okay.

CONGRATULATIONS

You have worked so hard and have come so far; please don't underestimate that. You are growing, developing and learning how to change your mindset through goal setting, visualisation and positive affirmations. *Well done,* congratulations. I liken this transformation to riding a bike for the first time. You're a little wobbly, and you may need stabilisers to stop you from falling off, but before you know it, you gain your balance through practice and repetition, and you're off free-wheeling through the park, feet off the pedals and legs in the air screaming 'Wooo-hooo!' However, what I would advise is, don't listen to those people calling to you from behind, just as your parents did when they would shout, 'Whoa, slow down! Be careful!' My advice is this: Keep pedalling like fury towards your vision and goal and what *you* want from *your* life. You are not on this earth plane to live your life for or through anyone else; it is *yours* to do with what you like.

I hope this little glimpse into my life inspires you to metaphorically grab the handlebars of your life and set off peddling, consciously and courageously, creating a more fulfilling reality for yourself and your loved ones around you. Life is a journey and not a destination. Enjoy every moment, every lesson, and every choice that is presented to you. If you're old enough to remember Jerry Springer, his final words on his show every day were always 'Take care of yourself and each other.'

KEEP IN TOUCH

I would be extremely happy if this book helped you understand and embrace the laws that govern our Universe so that you can experience a richer and happier reality. I would love to hear how this book has impacted or influenced your life. Please stay connected and sign up today for my free Newsletter, which covers other ways to enrich your life and embrace the Laws of the Universe, you can sign up here www.victoriagreen-lifecoach.com. You can also get in touch to share your experience at victoria@ victoriagreen-lifecoach.com

THANK YOU

My heartfelt thanks for buying and reading this book. I really do hope that you can intentionally implement all twelve laws to ignite a life full of purpose, love, and joy. I wish you every success and happiness. Remember: we are living this life now, so go out and make the most of it, AND have a ball doing so!

If I had my life to live over

I'd dare to make more mistakes next time.
I'd relax, I would limber up.
I would be sillier than I have this trip.
I would take fewer things seriously.
I would take more chances.
I would climb more mountains and swim more rivers.
I would eat more ice cream and less beans.
If I had to do it again, I would
travel lighter than I have …
I would start barefoot earlier in the spring
and stay that way later in the fall.
I would go to more dances.
I would ride more merry-go-rounds.
I would pick more daisies.

—Nadine Stair

THANK YOU FOR READING

Beyond the Stars: Embracing Cosmic Laws to
Intentionally Create a Life of Fulfilment!

I really appreciate all of your feedback and
I love hearing what you have to say.

I need your input to improve the next version of this
book and my future books.

Please take two minutes now to leave a helpful review on
Amazon, and let me know what you thought of the book:

Amazon.co.uk or Amazon.com.

Thanks so much!
Victoria

ACKNOWLEDGEMENTS

To My Mum, Christina:

Thank you for your unwavering belief in me and my abilities. I love you.

To My Son, Jamie:

What a journey we have had so far. I love you. You make me proud every single day.

To My Granddaughter, Isabella:

You are beautiful. You are amazing. You are my sunshine. You are enough, and you always will be. I love you to the moon and back.

To My Sister, Amanda:

Thank you for opening my eyes and showing me the light. I love you.

To My Eldest Niece, Ashleigh:

I am inspired by your free-spirited life, your bravery and your independence, and I love you.

To My Youngest Niece, Robyn:

You are a fantastic mum to Carter and Bobby; I admire the life, memories, and experiences you provide them, and I love you all.

To All My Friends:

You know who you are; I want to thank each of you for the love and support you have shown me throughout our friendship. No matter how short or long it has been, I appreciate and love you all.

Intellectual Debts:

I have learnt so much whilst writing this book through various media, and so I would like to thank all those who have imparted their knowledge via YouTube, published books and blogs, to name a few. You have contributed so much towards raising the planet's vibration, and with my small contribution, I hope to have achieved the same. Thank you to all those who continue to raise the vibration of the collective consciousness. Long may we bring about change and serve others. Love and light to each of you.

Last but Not Least

My heartfelt thanks, gratitude, and appreciation go to Jeannie Culbertson at www.noteworthymom.com, who has taken my words, polished them, and refined them into what you hold in your hands right now. She has been a professional guide and advisor every step of the way, and I couldn't have done this without her. Thank you, Jeannie.

ABOUT THE AUTHOR

Victoria Green was born in Dorset, England, UK. She later relocated to the North West of England as a child and grew up on the coast. She has a BSc in Physiotherapy and an MSc in Healthcare Leadership. She is an ICF accredited Life Coach, with a special interest in helping women manage their emotions during perimenopause and menopause. She is also an ABNLP Neuro Linguistic Master Practitioner, Quantum Healing Hypnosis Technique Practitioner, Reiki Practitioner, and now an author with a genuine passion for helping others.

When Victoria is not working, coaching, or writing, she enjoys walking on the beach with her beloved cockapoo, Dougal, or spending quality time with her family and friends. As a mother to one son and Nanna to one granddaughter, family is at the core of her life.

Victoria has dedicated much of her journey to personal development to create a fulfilling life for herself and her loved ones. She finds joy in assisting others in achieving similar transformations in their lives through coaching sessions.

Say hello and follow Victoria on social media:

Facebook: Victoria Green

Instagram: Iamvictoriagreen_coaching

If you want to work with Victoria, please visit her website: www.victoriagreen-lifecoach.com.

Printed in Great Britain
by Amazon